D0948619

BASKETBALL
Techniques, Teaching and Training

BASKETBALL

Techniques, Teaching and Training

BRIAN E. COLEMAN
National Coach
English Basket Ball Association

Illustrations by Roger Deer

KAYE AND WARD · LONDON

A.S. BARNES AND COMPANY
South Brunswick & New York

I would like to express my appreciation of the following people who have helped to make this book possible:

The many members of the basketball course I have had the pleasure to teach — their searching question have helped me in my thinking about the game; Roger Deer for the production of the illustrations — I have been very fortunate to have an artist who knows the game of basketball; the English Basket Ball Association for permission to reproduce the glossary of basketball terms — this glossary was originally published in *Coaching Basketball*, a guide for potential basketball coaches that I wrote for the Association; my wife, who besides helping me with advice on writing, has with her typing and correcting made this book possible.

First published in Great Britain by
Kaye & Ward Ltd
21 New Street, London EC2M 4NT
1975

First published in the USA by
A.S. Barnes & Co. Inc.
Cranbury, N.J. 08512, USA
1975

ISBN 0 7182 1085 9 (Great Britain)
ISBN 0-498-01712-5 (USA)
Library of Congress Catalog Card Number 74-24929 (USA)

Typeset in Great Britain by
Specialised Offset Services Limited Liverpool
and printed by Whitstable Litho
Straker Brothers Ltd, Whitstable

CONTENTS

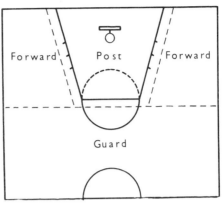

Forward Post Forward

Guard

DIAGRAM I

Key to the diagrams and symbols used in this book:

 Offensive player

 Defensive player

 Pass

 Path of the movement of a player

 Dribble

 Screen

Offensive Play — Front Court   Defensive Play — Back Court

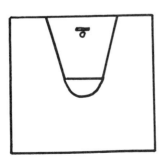 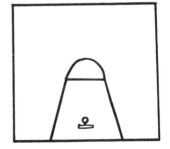

INTRODUCTION

This book is written from the background of a number of years as the National Coach to the English Basket Ball Association — a post that has involved travelling throughout England to organise courses on the game for teachers and coaches, and coaching players of various different levels of skill. This book sets out on paper much of the material covered at these coaching sessions. It is a book written for the teacher and the coach, and is intended as an introductory text rather than an advanced book on the game.

In writing this book it has been necessary to carry out some analysis of the game, and in carrying out this analysis on paper artificial situations have been created. Basketball as a game involves two teams, playing on the same area. Offence and defence cannot be separated; they are dependent upon each other. The simplification and division of the game into components for exposition in this book has a danger and the reader should remember that the 'part' is not more important than the 'whole'. From this book it is hoped that the reader will not only be able to learn the techniques and skills of the game, but will in addition gain an understanding of the game as a coherent whole. The book aims to help in the understanding of the game by emphasis on, and constant repetition of, a limited number of basic ideas which are developed through the book. Each component of the game has no easily recognised boundary lines and there is considerable overlapping and influence of one aspect of the game on another.

Most of the chapters in the book have been written along the lines of the title of this book, covering techniques, teaching and training. Under the heading of 'techniques' the reader will find not only a description of the technique involved but also some of the more basic principles. Under the heading of 'teaching' advice on the teaching of some of the techniques, skills and team play have been included, and under 'training' advice on some suitable practices for club and school groups.

This book has been primarily written for British basketball and sets out to help the coach and teacher increase their understanding of the game. It does not set out to be the last word on the game or to cover all aspects of play — this would be an impossible task within the framework of one book. The game of basketball is continually developing and there is no one method of playing the game that will guarantee success. When reading of certain offensive moves in this book it may appear to the reader that the defender has no chance, and that the move illustrated leads to a score every time. This is not so. Not everything you attempt will work every time. The defenders may be cleverer than you think. The inter-dependence of offence and defence is one of the fascinations of the game. The situations during a game are constantly changing. One movement affects another situation; indeed every movement of the ball alters the game situation.

Basketball is a simple game and the successful teams do the simple things very well. When the coach or teacher finds things are not working with his players, a quick answer to the problem is to simplify what is being attempted. This book has been written for the vast majority of clubs and schools in Britain. The generalisations that appear in this book do not take into consideration the many 'ifs', 'buts' and 'maybes' that would be necessary if the full picture were to be stated.

Although the illustrations in the book show men playing, the material covered in this book is equally appropriate for women and girls.

Like most sports basketball has its own jargon and a glossary of terms is included as the last chapter. Three terms are defined at this stage to aid understanding; these are the three terms that identify the three basic playing positions — Guard, Forward and Post. These terms are employed to identify the offensive position occupied by a player; the player's position will depend upon the area of court he plays in when on offence. Diagram 1 shows these areas and the name given to a player who occupies one of the positions.

INITIAL TEACHING AND COACHING

Basketball is a simple game and therefore in its basic concept it can and should be played immediately with a group of beginners with little introductory teaching other than an explanation of the basic ideas involved.

Basketball is primarily a team passing game, played with the hands, with the object of scoring a goal in a horizontal target which is 18" in diameter and suspended 10' from the floor. It is played to three basic rules: no contact, no running with the ball and one dribble. The early game played by beginners may to a purist look like disorganised chaos; it may be played three, four, five, six and even seven a side. The individual skills of beginners may be very limited, possession changes frequently and few baskets will be scored. The important thing is that from the moment they start playing the beginners are playing basketball. The teacher has only to find the time to organise a group into two teams, time to tell the beginners the three basic rules and time to bring them together to start the game with a jump ball at the centre. The teacher can do a great deal to improve the game of these beginners through coaching during this early game. To help the teacher in this early coaching this chapter will concentrate attention on two areas: the rules and the game.

THE RULES

The original thirteen rules, written out by Dr James Naismith for the first game in 1891, have changed considerably over the years; they have been defined in more detail and added to for international competition so that when two foreign countries play each other, for example USA and USSR in an Olympic final, the disputes about the exact meaning of the rules are kept to a minimum! The full International Rules would be totally unsuitable for use with a group of beginners; it is preferable that the rules they are given should be kept as simple and as few as possible to facilitate a game.

The three basic rules of playing the game have already been mentioned; these are, no contact, one pace and one dribble.

One Pace

Naismith's original rule limiting running with the ball has been more strictly defined and today a player is limited to one pace whilst holding the ball. A player is permitted to pivot, i.e. a movement when 'a player who is holding the ball steps once or more than once in any direction with the same foot, the other foot called the pivot foot being kept at its point of contact with the floor'. With beginners the rules concerning footwork should be fairly liberally interpreted. Provided the player does not run with the ball and endeavours to remain on the spot where he caught the ball no infringement of our basic rule of no running with the ball should be penalised. Any attention that the teacher gives to footwork in the early games should be directed towards achieving balance and control of the player, and as will be seen below this will involve teaching the pivot.

No Contact

The no contact rule is the most important and the teacher should endeavour to apply this rule strictly with his beginners, for without application of this rule the game degenerates into indoor rugby and the players will have no opportunity to develop their skill. Strict application of the no contact rule will enable the beginner to develop confidence in handling the ball. To discourage unnecessary contact the teacher should condition the beginners' game by preventing an opponent from gaining possession of the ball by taking or knocking the ball from the hands of a player who has obtained possession.

This will prevent the early game from becoming minor scrimmages around the ball and prevent the fore-arm smash and hacking that leads to so much contact.

One Dribble

The third basic rule of the game of basketball is concerned with the dribble. Most people who play basketball for the first time are aware that the game permits you to bounce the ball and move with the ball under control from one spot to another. By the rules of the game this is a continuous bouncing action using either hand, but not two hands simultaneously. The dribble ends when the ball is caught in one or two hands. Any number of bounces and steps can be taken and the dribbling .hand may be changed. Once the player stops the dribble he is not permitted to dribble again until the ball has been touched by a team-mate or an opponent. The basic rule is that a player is allowed one dribble (a dribble being a continuous bouncing action). With beginners and inexperienced players, who are unable to control themselves and the ball while at the same time looking at team-mates and opponents while they dribble, the dribble can become a limitation. With beginners the dribble usually becomes a 'head-down-one-player' action and thus limits the development of the game. The teacher working with a group of beginners may be tempted to abolish the dribble from the game entirely, playing basketball with the beginners as a team-passing game. He may reason that because the beginners are unable to dribble correctly then he will not let them dribble at all as it 'spoils' the game. The danger with this policy is that unless the beginners are permitted to dribble they will have no chance to learn *how* and *when* to do so. The teacher working with beginners is advised to *occasionally* condition the game by ruling out dribbling but to be more concerned that his pupils learn when to dribble, and he should incorporate instruction in dribbling early in his teaching programme.

RULES OF ADMINISTRATION

The teacher will have to introduce the rules concerning starting, stopping and restarting the game and ball out of play — rules that could be called the rules of administration.

The game is started with a jump ball at the centre between two opponents. When the ball goes out of play it is brought back into play from the nearest point at the side line by the opponents of the team who caused the ball to go out of play.

Basketball differs from other major team games in that it has no basic off-side rule at the start of the game, other than the fact that only the two jumpers are allowed in the centre circle at the starting jump ball. The non-jumpers can stand anywhere on court. The game is then started by a jump ball between two opponents. After a basket is scored the game does not return to the centre, but the ball is brought into play by the team who have had the basket scored against them from out of court at the end line under their own basket.

When violations of the basic rules of the game occur (i.e. no contact, one pace and one dribble) again basketball differs from other major team games in the way in which the game will be restarted. The basis of the restart rule is that the ball is awarded to the opponents of the player who committed the violation; they bring the ball into play from out of bounds at the nearest point at the side of the court to where the infringement occurred.

OTHER RULES

The International Rules book contains ninety-two articles. According to these rules free-throws are awarded for certain fouls. There are a number of time limitations in the game, for example a team has only ten seconds in which to move the ball from their back court (defensive half) to their front court (attacking half). Also, when a team has control over the ball, a player of that team may not remain in the restricted area for longer than three seconds. There are rules concerning playing the ball above the level of the ring. There are technical fouls to penalise players for ungentlemanly behaviour. Technical fouls, the three-second rule, the ten-second rule and the like should be ignored at first and only be introduced as and when the game requires them. The three-second rule should, for example, be introduced when attacking players realise the advantage in a no-contact game of 'goal hanging'. The number of rules introduced will depend upon the type and ability of the group being taught, on its previous experience of the game and the timing of its first competitive game. The teacher should err on the side of introducing the minimum number of rules to his group of beginners, thus allowing them to get on with playing the game without frequent interruptions.

COACHING IN THE EARLY GAME

The aim for the teacher when introducing the game to a group of beginners should be to start them playing a game and to maintain their enjoyment in this playing by improving their performance. The beginners' game will be all action, frequent changes of possession, attacks moving up and down the court — a picture of non-stop activity, crude to the purist but fun to take part in. The teacher has to step into this play, maintain the enjoyment and isolate those aspects of the game to be improved. Where does the teacher start? In front of him his group of beginners are endeavouring to play basketball. In these early stages the following sections will provide him with material that he can utilize to improve and, when necessary, to correct the appropriate skills.

Defending

The simplest defending situation in any team game is for one defender to be responsible for marking one opponent and continue to mark that opponent throughout the game, maintaining the defending responsibility wherever the opponent goes while on attack. In basketball every player on attack can shoot to score and can, within the rules of the game, use the dribble to move from the spot where the ball was received to a point on court closer to the basket. However, the player dribbling the ball is not permitted to barge a defender, who has established his defensive position, out of the way. Basketball is a no-contact game and every player is charged with the responsibility of avoiding contact. Because of these factors the defender endeavours to maintain a position on the court between the opponent and the basket he is defending. This is the basic defensive position in basketball, i.e. between opponent and the basket, and is preferred to a position ·between opponent and the ball because in these circumstances the opponent may receive the ball and be in a position to dribble in towards the basket for a closer shot. This is of course the most important use of the dribble to stress with beginners. Figure 1 (p.12) shows a game in which the defensive players have taken up this basic defensive position between opponents and the basket they are defending.

Safe Passing

Basketball is a no-contact sport and in theory it should be possible for the team in possession of the ball to retain possession. The teacher with his group of beginners will notice the frequent changes of possession. What is going wrong? The basketball is large and should therefore be held in two hands to gain maximum control. A useful maxim to apply is: catch the ball in two hands, pass the ball with two hands, be behind the ball when you pass it, and get yourself behind the ball when you catch it. With beginners the teacher should stress controlling the ball. In a no-contact sport the players have more time in which to control their movements, to control their passes and to think what they are doing. They do not have to be concerned with the impending tackle. As was mentioned earlier, the teacher is recommended to condition the game and prevent the defenders taking the ball from a player who has gained possession of it. The beginners are therefore encouraged to stop and think, and any time rules that may exist in the international game would not be applied to beginners. Basketball is mainly a short passing game, with the safe passing range for beginners being between 10 and 15 feet. At this range the passer can make short, sharp passes and he can see clearly if a team-mate is free and ready to receive the ball. The lob passes and long passes which give opponents time to move in and intercept should be discouraged and the teacher could well condition the early game to involve only passes that travel below head height.

Earlier it was suggested that with beginners the footwork rules should not be strictly applied. The teacher has to find a balance between having the young players running with the ball (against the rules) or being 'wooden' legged because they are trying not to run. Early in their learning of the game and developing out of the idea that the pass is only made when the team-mate is ready, the teacher could use the maxim: pass where you are looking; see where you are passing. This looking can be interpreted with the beginners as 'looking' with the feet. To be in the most favourable position to pass to a team-mate the player with the ball should be facing the team-mate with his feet pointing in the direction of the team-mate. To achieve this position the player with the ball may have to 'pivot', i.e. keep one foot at its point of contact with the floor, while moving the other foot. The pivot is thus used to face the potential receiver and to regain balance should the player with the ball have lost his balance. The teacher working with beginners should stress this control and balance prior to passing, as this will result in safer passes.

Being in a position ready to pass will improve passing; the teacher should, therefore, encourage the passer to hold the ball ready so that no preliminary movement is made prior to passing. Beginners tend to hold the ball low — at waist level; they should be encouraged to hold the ball high — that is up in front of the chest below the level of the chin, or above this height.

Team Spacing

When beginners play any team ball game for the first time they will all tend to chase the ball. Basketball being a small team game (five a side in the International Game), this may appear to be less of a problem than in Association Football, where 20 (or is it 21?) youngsters can be chasing one ball! The spacing of players on the relatively limited area of the basketball court is as important as in other team games. The distance between attacking players should be such that the defenders are required to mark on a one-to-one basis, that one defender cannot mark two opponents, and that the distance between the attacking players is such that they can make safe passes and catches. The receiver needs time to watch the ball so that he can make a safe catch, but this distance should not be so great that the defender has time to move in to intercept the pass. The safe passing range has already been given as 10-15 feet apart and this range should be used for team spacing. It forces the opponents to mark one-to-one, it facilitates safe passing, and the distance between attacking players allows room for the individual attacking player to execute drives (aggressive dribbles towards the basket) and cuts (moves without the ball) past an individual defender with less chance of other defenders being able to assist — assistance that is so easy when the players are bunched up.

Pass and Move

A simple and basic instruction to the attacking player in all team ball games is: pass and move into an open space. Basketball is not different from the other ball games in this respect. Players should pass and move looking for the return pass. Obviously, if the team is well spaced out on attack, there will be more room for a player to pass and move into a new position for the return pass. The teacher working with a group of beginners should emphasise that the open space that they should move towards for the return pass is the basket. The pass and move therefore become a pass and move to the basket looking for the return pass.

Space in the Area Under the Basket

If the players on attack are spread out, 10-15 feet apart, looking for a pass to a team-mate and an opportunity to move to the basket for a return pass, it will be useful if the area of court under the basket is kept free of attacking and defending players. The attacking team should aim to organise their spread to give them a spacing of players that will keep the under-basket area free, so that the player who passes and moves in for the return pass will find (when he receives the return pass and provided he has lost his own defender) that he has a relatively uninterrupted shot at goal. The teacher can help his players create this free space in the under-basket area if he stresses close man-to-man marking by the defenders, the appropriate spacing on offence, passing and moving for the return pass. If the player who has moved for the return pass does not get the ball he should move out from the under-basket area to allow another team-mate to move in. Should the defenders congregate in the under-basket area they will create a very effective defence against beginners, as the inexperienced players on attack will need to reach the under-basket area in order to have much chance of success with their shooting. When the vast majority of games end with each team scoring over fifty points, basketball is a game of attacking success, and the teacher should endeavour to create a situation in which the beginners on attack have a great deal of attacking success, which for them will mean shots at the basket. The beginners will enjoy this success and the teacher should organise his teaching to give attacking success before he is concerned with teaching a system of defence (e.g. a zone defence which may involve congregation in the under-basket area) that would prevent the attacking team's success.

Shooting on the Run

The attacking player may find himself moving to the under-basket area with the ball after a dribble past an opponent. The beginner will be tempted to stop under the basket and take his time with his shot. Unfortunately this will give defensive players a chance to recover and be in a position to harass the shooter. In basketball a player is allowed to occupy any position on the court not occupied by an opponent, provided that in moving to that position the player does not cause contact. The players occupy the piece of floor they are standing on (feet approximately shoulder-width apart) and the elliptical cylinder round their feet and up to the ceiling. The defender, if given time to recover, is permitted to stand very close (no contact) to the shooter and raise his arms above his head to discourage the shooter from scoring. Although it is recommended with beginners that they are not permitted to take the ball from an opponent who has gained possession (this is a condition that is recommended to help the beginner and inexperienced player have a more enjoyable early game), stealing the ball from an opponent is permitted in the full game. Because of these factors the attacking player moving into the under-basket area to take a shot should take the shot as quickly as possible. This will involve shooting on the move without stopping to take the shot. This shot on the run gives a quicker shooting action and the teacher should encourage his beginners to employ this shot. It is usually called a 'lay-up shot' and details of the technique of the shot and suggestions on teaching it are covered in chapter 2.

Control

Mention has already been made of the player being under control and on balance when passing. Watching beginners and inexperienced players, it can frequently be said that they appear to be running around and getting nowhere very fast. The fact that basketball is a no-contact game will mean that players have more time in which to control their actions on court and, when the game is played properly, there will be phases of deliberate play interspersed with phases of rapid play. Compared with contact sports the tempo of play in basketball will vary considerably. Inexperienced players frequently endeavour to play basketball at a speed that would be beyond the capabilities of the international player. Most beginners and inexperienced players play basketball too fast — too fast to control the play in order to analyse adequately what team-mates and opponents are doing and thus to make decisions about the next move. The teacher has to strike a balance between too much movement and too little. Earlier mention was made of the player, after passing, moving towards the basket for a return pass. Taken to its logical conclusion this could lead to a game of constant passing and moving. Obviously some players after passing will find themselves well marked and will not be in a position to move free after their pass. Other players will pass and move but not receive the return pass — either they do not get free, or the team-mate is marked and unable to pass. (Remember a pass should only be made if the passer can make the pass successfully.) The teacher should err on the side of having the player pass, move, and see if this leads to a chance for the return pass and shot. If it does not, then the player who has moved to the under-basket area should be given time to move out before starting the next pass and move action. Rather than have one player hold onto the ball while the original cutter (player moving without the ball) has left the under-basket area, the players should be encouraged to pass the ball without looking for opportunities to move in to score. Movement in basketball should be looked upon as movement of players (moving to spread out), movement of the ball (passing the ball between the attacking players), and movement of players and ball (player moving towards the basket to receive a return pass). The teacher has to find the right balance for his group. *Control* should be his watchword. Are the players under control? If they are, they will be in a situation in which they can learn.

Simple Tactics on Attack

The player with the ball is the only player who can score. He should therefore be encouraged to see if he can score every time he receives the ball by pivoting and *looking ahead* towards the basket he is attacking. Should he find that there is no one between him and the basket, the player should make use of the dribble to move to a position for a closer shot at goal. If, on facing the basket, the player finds that he is marked he will be looking in the appropriate direction to see if there is a team-mate in a position closer to the goal to whom he can pass. He can then *pass ahead.* Having passed, the attacking player's basic instruction has been to move towards the basket looking for the return pass. He should, therefore, after passing ahead, consider *moving ahead.* The attacking player, if marked when he received the ball, could well find that when he passes the ball to a player ahead of him the defender who is marking him, being unable to watch both ball and man, will be tempted to turn to see where the ball has gone. At this moment the attacking player, who has just made the pass, is free and should cut in towards the goal for a return pass. In figure 1, if the player with the ball (the right guard) passes the ball to his team-mate (right forward) who is signalling for the ball on the right hand side of the free throw line, the defender marking the passer could be tempted to turn his head to look at the ball, thus giving the right guard a chance to cut for a return pass towards the free area under the basket — an area left free because the attacking players are spaced 10-15 feet apart.

The simple tactic on attack that should be emphasised to the players is:

LOOK AHEAD
PASS AHEAD
MOVE AHEAD
SPREAD OUT

FIGURE 1

TEACHING

The teacher should aim for enjoyment and participation. A teacher working with a class of thirty children in a school gymnasium could initially introduce basketball with the whole class involved in playing the game if, instead of using the main court down the centre of the gymnasium, he divided it into three playing areas and the games were played across the width of the teaching space. In addition to the main court with two overhanging backboards down the centre, a well equipped gymnasium for teaching basketball should have six practice baskets. These practice baskets could either be small portable backboards (4 x 3 feet) with ring and attachments on the rear of the board to fix to window ladders or wall bars, or they could be permanently fitted small backboards with rings. Without a ring the teacher can improvise with chalk marks on the wall, painted targets or plastic hoops fixed to the wall bars or window ladders.

TRAINING

Suitable practices to use are:

1. Team Passing

Two teams are selected and the object of the game is to keep possession of the ball by accurate passing between team members. No shots are made and players should not dribble. Normal rules apply. The opposing team gains possession of the ball by intercepting a pass and/or when the attacking team drops the ball. This game can be varied and a score can be kept of the consecutive passes made by one team prior to interception or loss of the ball. The teams endeavour to beat the previous highest score of the total number of consecutive passes without an interception.

2. Full Game

The full game of basketball can be played when working with a small group of beginners. In using the full game for practice purposes it would be usual for the teacher to impose certain conditions on the game to focus attention on one particular aspect of the training game: for example, to impose the condition of no dribbling focuses attention on passing. Most coaches make use of the full game for a part of their training sessions to enable their players to put into practice in a game the particular aspect of play that has been emphasised during the training sessions. If the team has been working on their offensive play against man-to-man defence, obviously the condition to impose would be that the defence used in the game be man-to-man marking.

With beginners the teacher will, when playing the full game, be stressing the points made in the section on coaching in the early game (Chapter 1).

3. Half-court Basketball

A newcomer, watching a game of basketball for the first time, would notice that the game is mainly played around the two baskets — all ten players go down to one end of the court while one team develops their attack and then, on the change of possession, all ten move down to the opposite end of the court. A useful training game which eliminates the transfer of play from one end of the court to the other is a half-court game of basketball. In this game both teams aim to score into the same basket. To prevent this leading to a mad scrimmage under the basket the game is started by one team from the mid-court line. Once the game starts the normal rules of basketball are played until the ball is lost by the team on attack either by shooting and scoring or by loss of the ball through a mistake or violation. On gaining possession the team that was on defence brings the ball back to the centre line and then the players attack the basket that they have just been defending. The time that they take to bring the ball out gives their opponents time to take up defensive positions.

A slight variation of this game is for the team on attack to retain possession of the ball if they score, bringing the ball out to the half-way line before starting a new attack.

Another variation of half-court basketball is for the team initially on attack to have a specified number of 'lives' — say five or seven. When they shoot and score, shoot and fail to gain the rebound, or lose the ball through a violation, bad pass, etc., they lose one of their lives. After the set number of lives has been played, the teams change from attack to defence and the new attacking team endeavours to score more baskets than their opponents in their set number of lives.

4. Three versus Three

Half-court basketball can also be played three versus three or, in fact, any other suitable number selected by the teacher. The teacher can set particular conditions and the method of play.

2

INDIVIDUAL SKILLS

Basically there are four things that you can do with a basketball; they are: catch it, pass it, dribble it and shoot for basket. This chapter will consider these four individual skills. Before isolating these individual techniques for study, we would remind the reader that any individual technique must be considered within the context of the full game of basketball and this involves team-mates and opponents. In working with his players the coach should be aware of the underlying principles rather than the detail of technique. Different coaches will emphasise different variations in technique. We have endeavoured to limit the techniques described and would stress instead the principles, concepts and basic ingredients. The order in which the individual techniques are covered in this book is not intended to represent any special emphasis. As the basic objective of the game is to score, this has been considered by some authors as the most important individual fundamental. Failure to maintain possession of the ball could prevent a team from taking advantage of their shooting ability, so the first individual skill we shall consider is passing.

PASSING

Since basketball is a no-contact game, possession of the ball and retaining possession to enable the team to free a player, allowing him to shoot at goal and thus provide a scoring opportunity, are important. The purposeful movement of the ball must be not only safe but also effective if the team is to gain ˙maximum (optimum) advantage from possession of the ball. Safe passing should not always be equated with effective passing because, although an effective pass will be safe, a safe pass may not be received in the most advantageous position or at the most advantageous moment. To be effective the pass must be taken by the receiver *when* and *where* he wants it. The time in the game for the receiver is as important as the position in which he received the ball. It is a poor pass if a player has moved, freed himself and then does not receive the ball until the defender has recovered; equally it is a poor pass if a player who is free receives the ball near his feet rather than at the position from which he can either pass on to a team-mate or take a shot. Good passing can lead to good shooting. The ingredients that are required in a good pass are:

1. Accuracy
2. Timing
3. Appropriate speed
4. Deception
5. Relevance to the game situation

Accuracy

Basketball is a game of constant action, with changes of position by both team-mates and opponents. The receiver will want to receive the ball at the right time and in the optimum position to enable him to execute his next move with the minimum of delay, be it a shot, start of a dribble or pass to a team-mate. The pass should be one that can be comfortably caught by the receiver. Thus the target area should be in front of the receiver at a point where he can comfortably reach the ball without bending, over-reaching or jumping. Accuracy will depend upon the passer having control of the ball prior to passing — without this, successful passing can be a matter of luck. Obtaining maximum control of the ball requires two hands on the ball; the contact being made on the ball by the fingers but with most of the palm off the ball. Excessive movements of the ball for the purpose of faking frequently lead to some loss of control over the ball or place the ball out of the most favourable position for passing. An opportunity to pass may only occur for a fraction of a second and it is essential that the passer has the ball under control to make an immediate pass. Swinging the ball around, placing it behind the back or between the legs, puts the passer in a situation where he will have to move the ball to a more favourable position for a pass and these 'tricks' are not usually effective from the attacking player's point of view. Accuracy will depend on the relative position of the passer and his opponent: the further away the opponent is from the potential receiver the more latitude the passer has in his target. However, this latitude must not be too wide, as the pass must be made to the team-mate bearing in mind what the latter is going to do next. Is he going to shoot, pass to a team-mate or drive past an opponent? If the potential receiver is cutting towards the basket for a shot he does not want to receive the ball below waist level or behind his back, as both positions could make scoring a goal difficult if not impossible. Equally a team-mate who is free and in a position for a shot wants the ball quickly and accurately so that he can start his shooting action immediately. Any delay because he has to reposition the ball due to the pass having been made to his knees would give the defender time to recover.

Timing

The importance of the pass being made at the 'right' time in the game has already been emphasised. Timing is the *when* of successful passing and highlights the importance of the second player in a successful pass. Passing is a two-man relationship — the passer and the receiver. Too often passing is considered only from the point of view of the passer, particularly by coaches who are more concerned with striving to achieve a 'model' technique in their players. The receiver has an important part to play in making a pass a success. It may be necessary for the receiver to move to a new position to free himself from an opponent before he receives the ball. In moving to his new position the receiver can help his team-mate by signalling with his hand(s) where he wants the ball. The potential receiver needs to be aware that his team-mate is in position and ready to pass before moving free to receive it. Beginners frequently expend a great deal of energy getting free when the ball handler is not in a position to pass; for example, when the 'passer' is dribbling the ball, the potential receiver may move free only to find that the passer needs time to pick up the dribble and by the time the pass reaches the potential receiver the defender has recovered and is able to intercept the pass. This awareness of the action of team-mates is important from the passer's and the potential receiver's point of view. Players at both ends of the pass should be aware of what is happening on court, and learn to anticipate the movements and actions of team-mates. The good passer will be able to anticipate how the game is developing and will learn to anticipate where he will make the pass, even before he receives the ball. He will be able to anticipate the actions of team-mates and defenders, and thus be able to make a well-timed pass to a team-mate. This pass will help the team-mate in making his next move.

For the passer to be aware of what is happening on court, so that he can anticipate the actions of his team-mates, he will make use of his peripheral vision. The good passer will use a 'distant stare' without focusing his attention on any one particular team-mate or opponent. The passer should be able to *see* the player to whom the ball is to be passed, but it should not be necessary for him to 'look' at the team-mate as this will advertise his passing intentions. A good player should aim to develop his peripheral vision so that he can see everything that occurs in the 180° in front of him and with a quick turn of the head 90° to right and left everything on court. The inexperienced player needs to develop his effective peripheral vision, which from the author's experience is less than an angle of 90° in front of him. The wider and more effective the player's peripheral vision the more aware he will be of what is happening on court, and the easier it will be as a passer to anticipate movements of team-mates and opponents, thus improving the timing of his passes.

Appropriate Speed

The 'weighting' of the pass is the next quality required in good passing. Obviously there is a continuum of possible speed at which the ball can be passed. At one end of the continuum the ball will be passed with maximum speed and the danger in this situation is that the receiver will not be able to control the ball; at the other end the ball is passed so slowly that the opponents have time to move in and intercept the pass. The more time taken by the ball to travel from passer to receiver the more time an opponent will have to track the flight of the ball and intercept it. To cut down the opportunities for an interception most passes should be made aiming for optimum maximum speed, that is the top speed for safe catching. Working on the premise that the shortest distance between two points is a straight line, this means players should aim in most cases for the pass to be direct in flight from passer to receiver. As the optimum receiving zone will be in front of the chest just under the chin and the optimum zone for controlling the ball the same point, the passer should aim to make the pass with as much force as is commensurate with safe catching and in a plane as horizontal as possible. The time taken for the pass will also depend upon the distance between the two players involved and experience shows that a passing range of from 10 to 15 feet enables the passer to make snappy passes and not give the defender time to react and intercept the pass (always assuming that the pass is made to the side of the receiver away from the defender and the timing of the pass is right). The fact that a slow pass takes time can be used by a player when passing to a team-mate moving to receive the pass. The passer may want to give the team-mate time to move to receive the ball and so the pass may be thrown to a team-mate on a fast break down court so as to give him time to move onto the ball as he goes. When making a pass to a tall player the ball may be lobbed. However, there are inherent dangers in slow bounce and lob passes, therefore they should only be used in the appropriate game situation. A good maxim for successful passing is: not too fast; not too slow; not too high; not too low.

Deception

Mention has already been made of the use of peripheral vision by the passer so that he does not stare at a team-mate and thus enable a defender to anticipate the pass. The passer should see, but not look directly at, the man he is going to pass to; the passer aims to develop a poker face that does not give his intentions away. Disguising passing intentions is usually thought of as the use of fakes or feints prior to passing. Experience shows that players reveal to opponents their intention to pass by staring at opponents or by making a preliminary movement such as: (a) moving the ball from below waist level to a higher position in front of the chest prior to starting the pass; (b) holding the ball in one hand and taking the arm back prior to passing; (c) taking the ball in two hands behind the head and using a soccer throw-on technique in passing. All these preliminary movements give the defender a chance to anticipate the pass, therefore players should be encouraged to: (i) hold the ball in two hands in a high position (just under the chin upwards, rather than between waist and shoulder height) and thus be ready to make an immediate pass; (ii) hold the ball in two hands, passing the ball *from* two hands rather than one; and (iii) keep the ball in front of the plane of the shoulders. It is the preliminary wind up, whether this be the soccer throw-on technique or the low rugby-type pass, that gives the passing intention away. The skilled player will not rely on complicated fakes to disguise his intentions, rather he will deceive the opponents by fast release of the ball. This fast release will depend upon the use of the wrist and fingers in making the pass with the minimum of preparatory arm movements. This snap release of the ball is a skill that takes time to develop. The coach should encourage a beginner to eliminate excessive movements of the ball prior to passing and emphasise the follow through with his hand or hands in the intended direction of the ball to give it additional speed and control of direction. An opportunity to pass may occur for a fraction of a second and it is essential that the passer has the ball under control to make a quick pass. Swinging the ball around means that it will have to be brought to a more favourable position for a pass and 'tricks' for deception are not usually effective from the offensive player's point of view. When movement of the ball is necessary prior to passing, when for example it is necessary to protect the ball from an opponent attempting to steal, the movement should be deliberate and purposeful so that a pass can be made without any additional preliminary movements. A pass may be started from a variety of positions: the ball may for example be held relatively low to make the opponent think the player is either about to dribble or to make a low level pass; then, as the opponent moves down to cover, the pass is made over his shoulder.

Relevance to the Game Situation

Safe passing depends upon an appreciation of the relative positions and movements being made by opponents and team-mates. This ability to 'read' the game must and can be developed. How often has the player who has made a pass that has been intercepted been told by his coach to open his eyes? It should be the coach's job to help the players open his eyes. The coach can help facilitate the understanding and selection of the important features of the picture presented to the passer by team-mates and opponents, and finally help the player in the selection of the appropriate action to be taken.

The passer should be encouraged to look for possible passing lanes. The stance taken by the defender marking the person with the ball will influence the possible passing lanes. There are three passing areas around an opponent: the ball can be passed under, over or round the outside. The positioning of the defender's arms will open or close certain passing lanes -- if he has both hands above his head it will be extremely difficult to pass over the top of this defender without making a slow pass, i.e. a lob pass that could be intercepted. However, the defender in this position has left other passing lanes free, which can be taken advantage of by the passer. If the defender is marking the passer closely it may be necessary for the latter to pass 'through' the opponent. The distance between the passer and the defender is important in this case; the closer the defensive player the less time he will have to react to the pass and, providing the passer disguises his intentions by not winding up, the easier it should be for the attacking player to make the pass. The passer should hold the ball firmly under control and should be encouraged to look at his opponent's arm position. Look for the gaps that are not covered and then fire the pass through a gap with the minimum of preliminary movement. This is the fast release that has already been mentioned under 'Deception'. However, if the defender is not very close to the passer, the defensive player has more time to react to the pass and greater care should be taken by the passer.

The passer must also be aware of team-mates' movements. Should a team-mate be moving close to the passer to receive a pass, then this will influence the weight of the pass: the closer the range of the pass the less force need be put into the pass. Players should learn to recognise the movements that their team-mates make when getting free to receive a pass and learn to act accordingly. The passer must also be aware of the positioning of opponents marking team-mates. In some cases the position of the defender may mean that the pass has to be made to the opposite side of the receiver from the defender. Some players are more capable receivers of the ball than others and the passer has the responsibility of ensuring that a pass is made that his team-mate can handle.

A long list of 'named' passes can be made and readers will be aware of the vast number of combinations that could be built up when it is realised that a pass can be made:

1.   Direct to the team-mate or via the floor.
2.   With one or two hands.
3.   To one side or the other, or over an opponent.
4.   Starting from any position — low to high (although usually in front of the plane of the shoulder).
5.   Standing still or on the move.

The skilled passer will make use of a vast variety of passes, but the less able players will be more effective if they limit the types of passes they use and concentrate on simplicity and effectiveness. The more commonly used 'named' passes are included in the technique descriptions that follow. These names are not intended to isolate a very specific pass but are general terms; 'Chest Pass' for example is a name given to any pass made with two hands from in front of the chest that goes direct to the team-mate.

✶ *Chest Pass*

This is a short-range (10-15 feet) two-hand pass made from in front of the chest to a team-mate who is free from an opponent. The ball is held at the chest in two hands with the thumbs behind the ball and the fingers along the side. The elbows are bent at the sides and are below the level of the ball, but not under the ball. The ball is passed directly to a team-mate by extending the arms, wrists and fingers in the direction of the intended flight of the ball. Just prior to starting the pass the wrists and fingers are cocked, and in passing the thumbs tend to move under the ball. The arms should follow through fully in the direction of the pass. This pass has become the basic pass of the game, because the ball can be released with the minimum of preparatory movements which might alert opponents. This pass can be made direct and fast to a team-mate when the defender is out of position, and is one that a player can soon learn to pin-point to a team-mate up to a distance of 15 feet away. The pass should be made in front of the team-mate to a position just under his chin — he is then in a good position to shoot, drive or pass quickly. With younger players who lack strength to push the ball the necessary distance from a stationary position, they can step forward as they make the pass, as illustrated in figure 2. However, this step forward should be eliminated as they become stronger and more proficient.

FIGURE 2

★ *Bounce Pass*

This is an effective pass to use when there is an opponent

between passer and receiver, particularly when this opponent is tall and has his arms up (as in figure 3). The pass can be made with one or two hands. For the two-hand pass the action is similar to that for the chest pass except that it starts from a lower level, i.e. at waist or hip level, and the ball travels to the team-mate via the floor. A skidding action of the ball is required rather than a big bounce. It should strike the floor nearer to the potential receiver than to the passer. This is a slower pass and therefore slightly easier for the defensive team to intercept. It is often over-used and it should not be used when it is possible to make a direct pass to the team-mate. It is almost impossible to throw this pass too hard. As the players' ability increases and they develop a passing action that makes use of a vigorous snap of wrist and fingers, they can use a one-hand bounce pass action. The one-hand technique enables the player to reach round the side of a close marking opponent. Note that the one-hand technique should not involve a wind up of the arm to make the pass.

FIGURE 3

 *Overhead Pass*

This is another direct pass; this time the ball is held high so as to create the passing lane. It is an excellent passing tactic for a tall player to use when passing over a smaller opponent and can also be used by any player when very closely marked. The ball is held in two hands overhead with the arms fairly straight and the fingers and thumbs spread behind the ball. The ball is passed with a vigorous snap of the wrist and fingers, making use of as little wind-up of the arms as possible. The fingers and wrist follow through as the pass is made (see figure 4). In using this technique, the ball should not be taken behind the plane of the shoulder and players should be discouraged from jumping when making this pass.

FIGURE 4

✱ *Short-range Passes*

Although stress has already been laid on players spacing themselves 10-15 feet apart, occasions will occur (as for example in some post plays) when players will move close together so that short range passes will be made. When making these short, close passes the 'weighting' of the pass should be stressed. Mention has been made of the optimum speed of the pass so that the team-mate can catch the ball comfortably. With passes made at close range 'sympathy' when passing between team-mates should be emphasised. The passer should control and protect the ball from efforts to steal by opponents.

In a post play the player creating the post will initially have his back to the basket; he should stand slightly crouched with weight evenly distributed and the ball held in two hands away from his body. This player, when passing to his team-mate, should aim to make a short, soft, easy-to-handle pass. This will be achieved if the ball is released by an action in which the ball is 'squeezed' out of the hands, so that is is easily handled by the receiver cutting close. During the squeeze or snap of wrist and fingers the passer should be imagining that he is placing the ball on a shelf — a shelf which is situated at above waist level — and the cutter takes the ball from this shelf.

This short-range pass, instead of being a two-handed, underhand, snap pass, may be made with one hand using a hand-off pass technique. After protecting the ball with two hands and just prior to making the pass, the passer holds the ball with one hand underneath and 'hands it off'. Just prior to being taken, the ball is snapped into the air for the cutter to take. There is a danger with this technique of the receiver catching the passer's hands as he takes the ball, thus fumbling it. Due to the danger of fumbles with close range passes, it is important to stress the timing and speed of the pass, the height of the ball, which should make it easy to handle, and the softness of the pass.

✱ *One-hand Flip Pass*

Reference has been made to the one-hand bounce pass and

the use of a vigorous action of the wrist and fingers in making that pass. In the general discussion on passing the importance of disguising the passer's intention was also stressed. Obtaining the power required to give the necessary distance to the pass is difficult when using a one-hand passing action without the pass involving a give-away wind-up action. Although a wind-up action may be necessary when making a long-range pass with one hand, it should be avoided if possible.

The skilled one-hand passer is capable of holding the ball in one hand and using only a vigorous action of the wrist and fingers to obtain the necessary distance for the pass. This vigorous action of the wrist and fingers can be likened to a flip of the ball. Most players, as they improve in their level of skill, should be capable of developing the use of a one-hand flip pass. The ball being initially held in two hands to give the control of the ball, it is then passed with a vigorous snap of the wrist and fingers of predominantly one hand. Players are likely only to use this pass with one hand — the right hand for the right-hand-dominant players — but it is important to develop this skill with both right and left hands.

⚡ *Passes for Length*

Although basketball is essentially a short-range passing game, there will occur occasions in the game when it is appropriate for the pass to be made at a range in excess of 10-15 feet. Of course the highly-skilled player can be expected to make many of the passes already mentioned at a range of over 15 feet. With less experienced players the passes most commonly used to obtain length are one-hand passes. These passes could be: the one-hand pass with flexed arm, often called the Javelin or Baseball Pass; the one-hand pass with a straight arm; and the one-hand underhand pass.

In the Javelin Pass the right-handed player takes the ball in two hands to a position above the right shoulder and turns his body, taking an evenly balanced stance with the left foot leading and his weight on the right foot. The pass is made with a bent arm action with the right hand behind the ball. As the pass is made the weight is shifted forward. The ball is thrown with a quick snap of elbow, wrist and fingers. This passing action with the elbow flexed gives control of direction over a distance. The pass is used to make a longer pass, to bring the ball quickly in bounds on a fast break and to initiate a fast break with an outlet pass following a rebound. The disadvantage of this pass is the time taken on the wind-up, which could give the opponents time to recover or to anticipate the move.

The one-hand pass made with a straight arm bowling action enables more power to be obtained, but with the sacrifice of some accuracy. The transference of the weight forward is the same as in the Javelin Pass. This pass can be a useful passing technique for young players and women who need extra power in order to obtain distance.

The one-hand under-arm action can also be used to obtain distance in a pass, with the ball being passed with a straight arm action and a long follow-through in the direction of the receiver. Any excessive lobbing of the ball in this pass should be discouraged.

Teaching Passing

The coach will be concerned with three points: to develop familiarity with the ball and confidence in handling the ball; to develop the use of the wrist and finger snap to pass the ball; and to develop the players' ability to make the appropriate decision based upon the game situation. The coach will need to balance his teaching so as to cover these three aspects.

After giving the beginner an opportunity to play the game, the teacher should focus attention on passing by splitting his class into smaller groups — three is the recommended number, so that a two versus one game can be played. Using the small group practices and games some of the important ingredients of good passing can be covered, for example receiver moving, accuracy of the pass, and appropriate speed of the pass. If the two-versus-one situation is set up in a formal manner, with the player with the ball on one side of the court, the defender in the middle and the potential receiver at the other side, experience shows that in this formation the beginners will be tempted to lob the pass over the defender. This pass gives the defender little chance and can be 'banned', thus forcing the player who is to receive the ball to move to create a passing lane. To this movement, which should be a natural run and not a side skip, the signalling for the ball can be added. If the potential receiver does not signal, then no pass should be made. Having created a passing lane free for the pass, the accuracy of the pass can be improved. So the teacher using the small group situation works through the ingredients of good passing covered earlier. Within this two-versus-one situation the players will be developing some of the decision-making skills of passing.

To develop confidence in handling the ball and the essential use of the wrist and fingers in the pass the teacher should make use of some practices where there is no defender. Some suitable practices for this are given below in the section on training.

In the two-versus-one game that has been suggested as an initial practice when introducing passing to beginners most of the passes will be made from a stationary position. Passing on the move, however, should not be neglected. This can be practised by the players running down the court passing the ball between them. This can be carried out in pairs or in threes. When passing on the move with a group of beginners stress should be placed on the use of a natural running action with no hops, skips or bounds, with a two-hand pass being made to a point in front of the team-mate so that he runs on to the ball. The teacher, when setting out to develop the ability of his pupils to pass on the run, should initially be concerned with the passing and, other than to ensure that they use a natural running action, he need not be concerned with the rules of the game at this stage. The players passing on the move will frequently 'travel', that is take more than the permitted one pace with the ball, due to poor passing from team-mates or lack of ability to handle the ball. As both these abilities improve, the teacher will find that the players make fewer travelling violations. The teacher should check that the players do not run too fast and that the movement is con-trolled.

The passing practice on the move will become a starting point for some of the practices that will be featured in the chapter on the fast break.

The teacher and the coach will find that nearly all basketball practices involve some passing, and, even if the coach is using the practice to improve another skill, he should check the passing. It is easy for the players to make poor passes when they are not involved in a specific passing practice session. This could lead to poor passing in the game. Most basketball practices should be looked upon as passing practices.

Training

Two versus one — Pig in the Middle

This is the practice that was recommended as the early teaching practice: two attacking players against one defender, who endeavours to intercept the ball. The player who makes the pass which is intercepted (or touched) changes places with the centre man.

Circle Passing

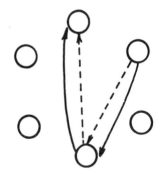

DIAGRAM 2

There should be at least six players in the circle. The players practise passes across the circle (diagram 2).

Variation — Pass and Follow

The player passes across the circle and follows the ball to where the pass is made.

Bull in the Ring

There are five players in a circular formation and one defender in the middle of the circle. The players on the outside of the circle endeavour to pass the ball across the circle, so that the

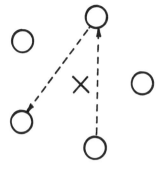

DIAGRAM 3

defender cannot intercept the pass. A player who makes a pass that is intercepted changes places with the defender in the middle of the circle (diagram 3).

A variation on this practice is to have two defenders in the centre of the circle with more players in the circle.

This practice can be made more challenging for the players by:

(*a*)   Disallowing passes between adjacent players.
(*b*)   Being strict on pass reception (clean catches).
(*c*)   Being strict on passes arriving on target.
(*d*)   Making the circle smaller.
(*e*)   Making the players on the outside circle change places with the defender when their pass is touched by the defender.
(*f*)   Forcing the players to make quick passes, no fakes, and the pass must be made as soon as the ball has been caught.

Shuttle Passing

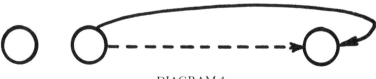

DIAGRAM 4

Two players stand one in front of the other facing the third player. The ball begins in the hands of the front man of the pair. The player passes to the one player opposite and follows the path of the ball, the new ball handler passes to the remaining one player on the other side and follows. The practice continues with pass and follow. Players should initially be spaced 10-15 feet apart.

A variation of this practice is to increase the number of players involved. Note that the ball should start from the side where there are most players. The players are in two lines on opposite sides of the court. After passing, the player runs to the end of the opposite line.

The type and length of passes can be varied. The passes can be made from a stationary position or on the move. When the passes are made on the move, they become shorter and the practice encourages the players to be sympathetic with their passing, i.e. passing at an appropriate speed for the team-mate to catch. When passing on the move stress should be laid on using a natural running action with no hops, bounds, skips or change of step when handling the ball.

Triangle Passing

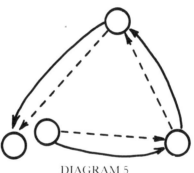

DIAGRAM 5

Four players form a triangle with two players, one with the ball, at one corner. The practice is for the player with the ball to pass to another corner and follow the pass to take the receiver's position. The ball is continuously passed round the triangle with the players breaking to a new position after the pass.

The direction of movement of both the passes and the players can be changed to add variety. When working with five players, this practice becomes passing and following around a square.

Circle Pass and Follow

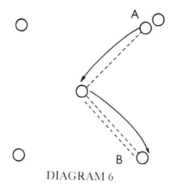

DIAGRAM 6

Players are arranged in a circle. If there are only six players (as shown above) the formation will be a square, with two players at one corner of the square (corner A), with one of these players holding the ball. In the centre of the circle (square) one player is stationed. The ball is passed from corner A to the player in the middle and the player follows his pass to take the middle position. The middle man on receiving the ball, turns and passes out to the player in the next corner (B), and he then follows his pass. The player in corner B passes the ball back into the middle, to the new middle man who made the original pass into the middle. Each passer follows his pass, the ball going from a corner to the middle, out to another corner and back to the middle, and so on.

When more players are involved more than one ball can be used. The number of players in the middle equals the number of balls being used; four balls are the suggested maximum.

Pepper Pot

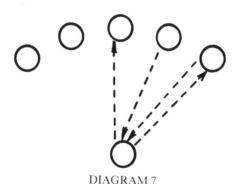

DIAGRAM 7

One player stands 10-15 feet away from four or five other players. Two balls are used. The player at the front and one other player in the arc each hold a ball. The player facing the line passes to any member of the line and, as he releases his ball, the second ball is passed to him. The two balls are moved continuously from the arc to the front man. Give the front man between 20-30 seconds pressure practice, then let another player take a turn, until all the players have been given an opportunity to be the front man. Emphasis should be on the use of wrist and finger action in making the pass, so as to improve the players' 'wrist snap' action.

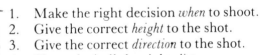

SHOOTING

Basketball is a high scoring game and an improvement in individual shooting ability pays dividends for any team. The ability to score a high percentage of shots taken, particularly within an 18 foot range of the basket, should be the aim of all players. In a club game of basketball between 30% and 40% of all shots taken in this range should be successful. In top class basketball players are now scoring over 50% of *all* the shots they take. As with the passes, there are a number of 'named' shots, but before considering these we will consider some of the underlying points regarding successful shooting. To score every time the shooter needs to get four factors right; these factors are:

1.   Make the right decision *when* to shoot.
2.   Give the correct *height* to the shot.
3.   Give the correct *direction* to the shot.
4.   Shoot the ball the right *distance*.

Obviously we do not expect a player to be able to score every time, but as the purpose of each team is to throw the ball into the opponents' basket, shooting could well be considered the most important fundamental. Basketball is a very simple game — all you have to do is to put the ball in the basket more often than your opponents. All great shooters, regardless of the technique they use, can be distinguished by one important fact, and that is that their tremendous shooting ability did not just happen suddenly. The great shooter will have spent many hours of practice to reach the standard of being a 60% shooter. Bill Bradley, an American who spent time at Oxford University in the 1960s and is now a top professional player in the United States, spent two to three hours per day, every day of the year, shooting as a schoolboy. Although the beginner may find shooting and scoring difficult in the early games he plays, improvement will come with practice and a coach should be able to guarantee to his players that they will improve their shooting ability the more they practise, assuming that the players apply the basic points mentioned above. These basic points will now be considered in more detail.

⚹1. *Height*

As the target is an 18 inch diameter ring placed horizontally at a height of 10 feet above ground level the shooter must aim to flight the ball so that the ball drops down through the basket. The flight path of any ball shot is a parabolic path and it is recommended that players aim for a medium arc on their shots with a release angle of near 45°, particularly for the longer shots. The technique used by the shooter for his shot should give the necessary lift to the ball so that it drops down into the basket, remembering that the ring is 18 inches in diameter and that the basketball is just over 9 inches in diameter. So a player is shooting a comparatively small ball into a large target. The optimum arc will be the one that enables the ball to enter the ring at a position as near vertical as possible, proportional to the lowest possible velocity of the ball.

⚹ 2. *Direction*

To throw the ball accurately requires control: control of the ball before commencing the shot and control of the flight of the ball along the correct line. Obviously the shooter must also know where the basket is and for this the shooter should concentrate on the target, be it the ring or a spot on the backboard, prior to taking the shot. For most shots taken in the game the target will be the ring; only with close to basket shots will the shooter aim to score by banking the shot off the backboard. A basketball player does not aim the ball by sighting and lining up ball and target — rather the player sights the target and guides the ball in the direction of the goal without looking at the ball. The player, when shooting for the basket, should imagine that the ring is a wooden shelf and then aim to drop the ball down onto the middle of this shelf. Concentration on the target should continue until after the ball has left the hands and is well on its way to the basket.

To be able to control the direction of the ball the players must have control over the ball throughout the shot and must co-ordinate the actions of the hands, arms and body to give the desired direction. To gain this control throughout the shot most shooters hold the ball in two hands. Here of course we have a link with other skills, for example, passing and catching. The stress laid on the use of two hands to control passing and catching is also applicable to shooting. However, the player is unlikely to use both hands simultaneously to shoot the ball. By using one hand to guide the ball the shooter overcomes the possible problem of co-ordinating the two hands, dominant and non-dominant. Most players use one hand, their dominant hand, to guide the flight of the ball. They do this by placing the shooting hand behind the ball (behind in relation to the target), with the other hand at the side to steady and support the ball. The two hands form a 'corner' in which the ball is held. The ball remains in two hands for as long as possible throughout the shot and for most shots the non-shooting hand is only released just prior to the final release of the ball in the shot.

A player taking a shot using one hand on the ball is likely to lose control over the ball and this style generally will only be used by players for shots close to the basket. Even then the player will still aim to maintain his grip on the ball with the shooting hand behind the ball. To maintain control over the ball for as long as possible the player will follow through with wrist, fingers and arms towards the target. The wrist, which is slightly cocked, and the fingers, which are spread comfortably but firmly on the ball, play a most important part in directing a shot. The player should be aware of the feel of the ball. Remember that as he does not line up eye, ball and basket, touch becomes vital. From the cocked position of the wrist the player follows through with a snap of the wrist and fingers. It will be easier for the player to obtain direction if the shot is taken along his line of sight. This is why some coaches tell their players to shoot the ball up their nose, which may put the elbow and wrist in a position which is not mechanically the most efficient to obtain distance, but from experience it has been found to be the most efficient action to obtain direction — distance being obtained through power generated by other parts of the body. To obtain control over the ball the shooter will keep the ball close but not up to the body and, until just prior to the release, keep the elbows flexed and close to the body.

A noticeable feature of good shooters is the vigorous snap of the wrist as the ball is released. From the cocked position with the wrist back, the shooter pushes his fingers through the 'middle' of the ball with a vigorous snap of the wrist. The wrist, starting in a cocked position flexed back, finishes after the release of the ball in a flexed forward position.

3. *Distance*

This is a matter of putting the appropriate amount of force into the shot. For a shot close to the basket this can be achieved by the use of wrist and fingers, as for example in a tip-in shot, but for the long set shot from 25 feet the distance will be obtained by starting the shot with a drive from the legs. With the shots that require longer distance the player must apply the force over a longer time and, of course, it is possible to apply more force the longer the feet maintain contact with the ground while making the shot. Should the feet leave the ground the player will continue to gain benefit from his jump provided the ball is released before the top of the jump. Should he postpone the release until he reaches the top of his jump or after, the player will then have to find the necessary force for the shot from his arms and shoulders. He will not gain distance from the drive of his jump by waiting till the later stage — in fact, this will make gaining distance for the shot more difficult. Obviously the way the player gains the necessary power for his shot will vary according to the distance from the goal. The way the player gains power for the shot should be considered as the result of the build up from toes to finger tips, with force being added by lifting the heels, straightening the legs, extending the arms and snapping the wrist and fingers. For the longer range shots this build up of power must be co-ordinated so that maximum force is put behind the ball.

It will obviously be easier to gain the necessary distance if movement by the shooter is up and down on the spot or movement towards the basket, at the same time transferring the weight forward. Movement off the straight line towards the basket will not only upset direction finding but will also dissipate force in the wrong direction.

The further the shooter is away from the basket the more he should use the drive from his legs to obtain distance. Straightening the legs on leaving the ground in following through will give the power necessary to obtain distance. The shooter should aim to use the drive upwards rather than forwards. Movement forward could lead to the shooter making contact with a defender which is a foul by the former.

4. *Appreciation of the Game Situation*

The player's ability to be aware of what is going on around him was stressed when considering passing and obviously with shooting it is again important. A player needs to know not only when to shoot but also when not to shoot. Players have to learn to recognise when an opportunity presents itself for a shot, as this will depend upon the position of opponents and team-mates, particularly team-mates who may be in a more advantageous position to take a shot. The potential shooter must learn to recognise honestly his own shooting ability and shoot when he is confident that he can score — this will obviously only come through practice. If a player feels that he can score, then he should take the shot. A player who is confident that he can shoot will be more relaxed in his shooting action. Unnecessary tension in the body will make it more difficult to get the direction correct. The good shooter will, having decided to shoot, concentrate on the task in hand and ignore defensive attempts to distract him. Watching the good shooter you will see relaxation, concentration and confidence. The more capable shooter puts the defender out of mind and ignores the defender's attempts to distract him when shooting. Obviously, if the defender's position is such that he is capable of blocking the shot after it has left the shooter's hand, then the shot should not be taken or the shooter should trick the defender out of position so that the shot can be taken. Ultimately the shooter's success will depend upon his ability to appreciate the position of the defender relative to his own shooting ability. Less able shooters will require more time, and time in this situation means room, i.e. distance from an opponent. As players develop in their shooting ability so they will be able to get the shot away faster. This speed of shooting is one of the reasons for the importance of the jump shot in modern basketball. This shot is used as much because the offensive player can 'get the jump' on the defender and shoot quickly, as it is used to gain height over an opponent. Quickness in shooting obviously should come as the player develops his shooting ability; speed for its own sake will be of no use if the player loses control of direction or height or, through shooting quickly, fails to apply sufficient force to the ball to obtain the necessary distance to score.

The quick shooter is the player who can get his feet into position and get the ball into a position for the shot quickly. A player should not take a hurried shot but, because he comes into a threatening position for the shot quickly, he becomes more effective.

A number of different 'named' shots can be identified and various styles of executing these shots noted. Although top-class international players may use a variety of shooting styles, it is possible to identify certain 'basic' shots. These basic shots form a foundation on which players can develop their shooting ability.

   Three basic shots can be identified; these are:

1.   Shots taken on the run close to the basket.
2.   Shots taken from a stationary position.
3.   The quick shot taken during a vertical jump.

These shots are usually called:

1.   Lay-up shot
2.   Set shot
3.   Jump shot

In addition three other shots may be noted: hook shot, free shot and tip-in shot.

⚹ *Lay-up Shot*

Usually the player taking this shot attempts to place his shooting hand as close as possible to the target before releasing the ball. Usually the shot is bounced off the backboard into the basket. The shot is used either by a player who cuts towards the basket, receives a pass on the run and shoots while moving forward towards the basket, or by a player who, having dribbled the ball towards the basket, gathers it from the dribble and shoots on the run.

The right-handed player (as illustrated in figure 5), using the shot at the end of the dribble, will gather the ball in two hands at a time when both feet are off the ground whilst running. The right foot is then grounded and the left foot becomes the take-off foot for the jump. The player jumps up towards the target, with a lift of the right knee as the jump occurs, and the ball is taken up in front of the body in two hands. As the ball is taken up, it is turned so that the shooting hand (right) is behind the ball with the other hand (left) at the side of the ball. The player releases the ball with the arm and hand at full stretch, aiming to lay the ball softly against the backboard so that it drops easily into the basket. The jump off the left foot should be a high jump, with the player endeavouring to convert his horizontal forward movement into a vertical lift, in order that the shooting hand on release of the ball is as close as possible to the target, so that the length of flight is as short as possible with the ball being released at the peak of the jump. The non-shooting hand remains on the ball until just prior to the release of the ball. The ball is kept close to the body throughout the shot to prevent an opponent making contact with the ball and upsetting the shooter. The fingers of the shooting hand are spread comfortably behind the ball and the player uses a wrist and finger action to lay the ball softly on the backboard.

This basic shooting action forms the basis of the shots made close to the basket that players will develop as they become more proficient. Skilled players frequently make use of a shot that combines some features of a lay-up and a jump shot. When playing close to the basket and finding that the defender has left a space between offensive player and the basket, the offensive player with the ball will jump through the gap, usually from a two-foot take off, and lay the ball up on the backboard. This shot involves the player jumping or sliding through a gap and, to give added protection to the ball, the offensive player will keep his back to the defender. The close shots can be taken with the left hand, or with both hands, with the shooting hand under rather than behind the ball, directly into the basket or off the backboard. The shot can be taken with a lay-back shooting action, which means shooting the ball from the opposite side of the basket from that which the basket is approached. The player goes under the basket and lays the ball back into it. He may use a type of hook shot, in which the ball is not taken up in front of the shooter but is held out to one side — the side away from the defender — and the ball is 'hooked' over the head of the shooter towards the target.

⚜ *Set Shot*

This is the shot taken by a shooter from a stationary position on court and used to gain distance for shots from 15-25 feet from the basket. Although the teacher should encourage a beginner to take the shot from close to the basket, as his skill develops the player should be moved further away from the basket. In senior club basketball a set shot from outside the 20 foot range is not uncommon and the ability to score consistently from the 15 foot plus range with this shot should be the aim of all players. The shooter stands facing the basket, one foot ahead of the other, on balance with the knees slightly bent, and the ball held in two hands in front of the chest just under the chin. The shot is started by straightening the legs and pushing upwards. The ball, as it passes in front of the face, is turned so that the shooting hand is behind and slightly under the ball. The non-shooting hand maintains contact with the ball to give it support. The shooting hand releases the ball, when the arm is fully extended, with a vigorous snap of the wrist and fingers — the finger tips being the last part of the

hand to leave the ball. The follow through with both hands and arms should be upwards and towards the basket. As the legs straighten, the weight should be transferred forward onto the foot corresponding to the shooting hand, thus a right-handed player will transfer his weight forward onto his right foot. The player should aim to maintain a continuous flow in his action from the moment he starts the shot until the release of the ball. The action illustrated in figure 6 indicates the positions the shooter goes through.

The follow through should bring the player up onto his toes and may even cause him to leave the ground with a slight jump after release. However, the player should not develop an excessive movement forward as this may upset his distance finding, or cause the shooter to close his distance from an opponent and perhaps make contact, thus fouling the defender. Some players start this shot holding the ball higher; this enables them to take the shot from a position closer to the defender without fear of the defender checking the shot. However, this is not a recommended technique as, from a position with the ball held high, it becomes difficult to apply the necessary force to give distance to the shot. This high starting technique also has the disadvantage that it takes longer to move the ball down into a dribble.

FIGURE 5

⚹ *Jump Shot*

This is the shot most used in the senior game today. Since its
introduction it has revolutionised the game of basketball as a
well timed jump shot is difficult to defend. A jump shot is a
quick shot taken after a vertical jump with the ball being
released near the apex of the jump. The shot may be made
from a stationary position, but it is more usual for a player to
take a jump shot after some movement. This movement may
be a dribble (see figure 7), the reception of a pass on the move,
or a pivot. The initial movement gives the player more
impetus for his jump. The player, prior to starting the shot,
establishes a balanced position facing the basket. Figure 7
illustrates the player turning to face the basket after a lateral
dribble. From this position he jumps upwards and, as the
jump occurs, the ball is taken up in front of the face to a
position in front of the forehead, with the shooting hand again
behind the ball and the non-shooting hand supporting the ball
at the side. From this position, with the payer now concentrating his sight on the basket under the ball, the ball is
flighted towards the basket with a vigorous wrist and finger
action and the shooting arm is extended just prior to the
player reaching the peak of his jump. The wrist and fingers
follow through in the direction of the basket. The player
should not strain to gain extra height so that he loses rhythm
and becomes tense in taking the shot.

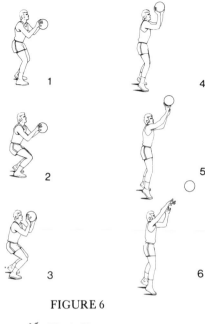

FIGURE 6

✳ *Hook Shot*

This shot is used by players in the area close to the basket. The shooter either makes his movement towards the basket when taking the shot or (see figure 8) the shot is preceded by an initial step away from the defender. The former is more of a driving lay-up shot with the shooting arm action slightly different from a lay-up shot. In the hook shot the ball is taken up to the side so that the body of the shooter protects the ball from the defender.

A hook shot used by a post player, who starts the shot with his back to the basket, can be a very effective shot and

FIGURE 8

FIGURE 7

extremely difficult to defend (see figure 8). The shot will be taken from a position relatively close to the basket, usually within the 15 foot range. The player, taking the shot from a stationary position in the key with his back to the basket, will usually preceed the shot with a fake. The player then takes one step away from the defender and, as he makes this step, he focuses his attention on to the basket. The ball starts in two hands from a position away from the defender, so that with the right-handed shooter the ball is held at the right side with the left shoulder pointing to the basket. The ball is shot with a sweeping action of the arm, starting at shoulder level with the arm slightly flexed. The arm extends and makes a smooth sweeping action to straighten as it comes overhead. The ball is released using the wrist and fingers, and the arm follows through towards the target.

FIGURE 8

Free Shot

This is the only shot taken during the game where the player takes it undefended. The player is allowed five seconds to take this shot. The majority of players use their one hand set shot when taking free throws during the game. Top-class players aim to score at least 70% of their free throws. The technique of the set shot has already been covered previously and all that need be added is to stress the importance of the players developing a routine for taking their free throws. This routine could be:

(*a*)   Dry hands and fingers before stepping up to the line, and shake the hands and fingers to release any tension.

(*b*)   Move up to the foul line.

(*c*)   Take the ball from the official, place the feet in position — this should be the same for all free throws. The position of the toe(s) should be such that the shooter does not step onto or over the line during the shot.

(*d*)   The player may bounce the ball a couple of times prior to shooting to relax the fingers and wrists.

(*e*)   Take the ball so that the fingers are comfortable on the ball and the player can 'feel' it.

(*f*)   Look at the basket. At this stage some players take a deep breath and exhale slowly.

(*g*)   Shoot the ball into the basket.

The players should aim to make their free throws mechanical in action and they should repeat the same action for each shot. It will be noted that in this routine it is not suggested that the player holds a shooting position for long. It will be found that if a player, when taking any shot during the game, holds the shooting position for too long tension is likely to build up in his body and he will lose the relaxation that is so important for success.

Tip-in

For any player who will be involved in offensive rebounding for his team a tip-in shot can form an important part of his shooting repertoire. The player does not have enough time in this shot to bring it under control and gain the correct position. Timing of the rebound jump is vital. The offensive rebounder must time his jump so that he can take the ball just prior to reaching the apex of his jump. The player, taking advantage of timing, height and reach, cushions the ball slightly with his wrist and fingers, with the arm at full stretch, and pushes the ball back into the basket softly on a low trajectory. As players find it easier to gain more height with one arm up, it is usual for a player to use a one hand tip-in shooting technique.

✗ *Teaching Shooting*

When teaching shooting to beginners the teacher should aim for *success* early on — success in mastery of a technique as in the lay-up shot, or success in scoring. With success will come pleasure and confidence, essential ingredients of any teaching situation.

Lay-up Shot

A game that should be used with beginners is a two versus one game, with the two players aiming to score. Unless the two attacking players can shoot on the run, the defender could well cover most of the shots they attempt. The shot on the run, or lay-up as it is called, should be taught to beginners early in their learning of the game.

It would be preferable for the teacher to demonstrate the shot to the beginners emphasizing the run, jump, and reach feature of the shot. The beginner should then have a go, either attempting the shot into the basket or, if he is in a large class, to a spot on the wall. The run, jump (one-foot take off), and reach form the basic pattern of the shot. While practising this pattern the teacher should check the control of the ball in the shooting action. The player should hold the ball with the shooting hand behind the ball and the non-shooting hand at the side. As the player moves forward and jumps, the ball is taken up in front of the face.

Having established the basic action and ball carriage, the beginner should be taught the rhythm of the shot. One method of doing this is to station the player five paces from the target — if this is the basket, he should be facing the basket at 45° to the backboard. From this position the player will run or walk forward, taking three paces prior to jumping and shooting. For right-handed players (the reverse for left-handed players), starting with two feet together, the footwork is left, right, left, jumping off the left foot and reaching up to aim the ball off the backboard from a point just inside the top of the small black rectangle painted above the basket. Again check that the ball is taken up in front of the face and that the beginner starts with the shooting hand behind the ball. Once the player has mastered the left-right-left with a jump and reach to lay the ball against the backboard, the dribble should be included. This can take the form of repeating the earlier pattern of movement but with the player bouncing the ball once as the first left foot step is taken in the three pace rhythm. The ball is picked up by the player after this initial one bounce.

The player is now using a bounce, one (right foot), two (left foot), rhythm to execute the shot. Once the rhythm of the shot has been mastered by the player working alone, the next step is for the ball to be passed to him as he· moves forward. Initially this pass may be no more than a hand-off, with the ball being held on one hand by a team-mate so that the beginner repeats the movement he has just learnt and takes the ball at the same point in the movement as he would have picked the ball up after the one-bounce dribble. As the player increases in skill so the length of the pass is increased. As this occurs, the shooter will take more steps in his run up to take the ball, although still approaching the basket at 45°. A practice using three players is illustrated in diagram 8. The

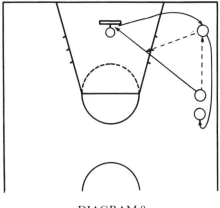

DIAGRAM 8

player passes the ball to a team-mate in the corner and cuts in to the basket for the return pass and the lay-up shot. After taking the shot the player gathers his own rebound and passes back to the team-mate waiting for his turn. The player in the corner, after passing to the shooter, joins the end of the waiting line and the shooter, having passed out after the rebound, goes to the corner.

To increase the level of their skill the players will need to practise taking the shot starting from different positions on court, e.g. after a dribble of different length and direction, against an opponent, and from passes received from varying positions on court. The method of teaching the shot using the bounce, one-two action is recommended because this rhythm is the pattern taught to beginners when they learn to beat a defender — one versus one when the defender makes the mistake of stepping forward.

A lay-up shot following a pass from the corner is a method of developing the give and go, which is an offensive move for freeing a player for a shot which is covered in chapter 5.

Set Shot

When learning a set shot, the beginner should start close to the basket. The starting position taught for this shot should be one foot in front of the other, and both feet comfortably spaced apart, with the same foot as the shooting hand forward. The knees should be bent and the ball held in front of the chest just under the chin. From this position, starting with the drive up from the legs, the ball is driven and guided up to drop into the basket. The follow through with arm, wrist and fingers should be emphasised, so that the shooting hand and arm could be said to aim to 'reach to put the ball into the basket', whilst the wrist and fingers should 'push through the middle of the ball' or 'wave the ball goodbye' as it goes to the basket. After the release of the ball the shooting arm should finish extended *upwards*. Once the beginner succeeds, he should step one pace back from the basket. Progressing in this way he is then shooting from a position from which he will have confidence in his ability to score.

As the level of the skill increases the player will be gradually shooting further from the basket. The teacher should check that the shooter is still achieving success — a successful rate being to score three or four out of every ten shots taken. With the increase in skill, a defender should be introduced, passive initially and then active. Once the defender becomes active, the attacking player must combine other facets of one versus one attack with the set shot (see chapter 3) and should be permitted to make use of a drive past the defender to take a lay-up shot.

Jump Shot

We would recommend that a jump shot should be taught after the players have developed some proficiency with a lay-up shot and a set shot. As with a set shot, the pupil will be positioned close to the basket when initially learning the jump shot, so that success is easier.

The learner should stand with feet apart, one foot in advance of the other. The rear foot is moved so as to bring the feet parallel, alongside each other but not together. This gives a wider balanced base. From this position the player jumps up from two feet, landing at the same spot as at take-off. This gives a step alongside and jump action. As the jump is started the ball, held in two hands, is swung up in front of the face to a position above the forehead. The player focuses on the basket under the ball. Figure 7 illustrates this pivot forward, jump from two feet and swing of the ball up to the shooting position. From this position, with the ball above the forehead and the player nearing the top of his jump, he shoots the ball to the basket. The timing of the shot should be jump and then shoot, not jump and shoot in one action. A skilled player taking a jump shot often appears to hang in the air before shooting. Most beginners shoot too early and the teacher should over-correct this fault by telling him to wait until the top of the jump before shooting.

A jump shot should be practised so that the player becomes proficient in executing the shot with either right or left foot as the forward foot. The player should also execute the shot after a one bounce dribble as in figure 7. Finally practice should be given in the execution of the shot with a jump shot after receiving a pass from a team-mate.

Hook, Tip-in and Free Shot

Teaching a hook shot and tip-in shot will only occur after the player has gained skill in the use of the other shots. The hook shot can be developed out of a lay-up shot. A tip-in shot can be included in the learning programme of the rebounding skills. As for a free shot the players have been recommended to use their basic set shot technique and as they develop skill in a set shot from 15 feet so they will be developing ability to take free throws.

Training

As has been said before, most basketball practices will at some time become passing practices. As most practices will include a final shot at goal shooting practice will feature in other training routines. The practices that follow focus attention on shooting.

Two File Lay-up Practice

This is a familiar basketball practice with two files: one shooting file A and the other, the rebounding file, B. The practice starts by the front player from file A taking the ball,

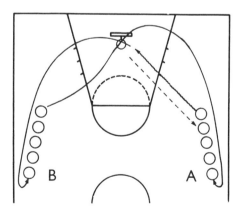

DIAGRAM 9

driving into the basket and shooting. The first player from file B moves in to retrieve the ball or take the rebound. He passes the ball out to the next player in File A, who repeats the operation. After shooting, the player joins the back of file B; after rebounding and passing out, the player joins the back of file A.

The practice should also be carried out from the left-hand side or with the shooter moving down the middle. With this practice the files tend to creep in towards the basket. The coach should check this and ensure that the rebounder runs in behind the driver and endeavours to gain the ball before it touches the floor.

A variation on this practice is to use two balls, both starting from the shooting file, with the second shooter moving in as the first shoots.

A further variation of this practice is for the player from file A, who is to shoot, to cut in to the basket, receive a pass from the rebounder and then go through for the shot without using a dribble. If this variation is used, the timing of the cut and the weighting of the pass out become important contributory factors. However, this practice is practising a movement (cutting in for a lay-up shot and taking a pass from under the basket) that is seldom or never used in an actual game. An improvement of the practice, that will make it more realistic, is for the rebounder, after taking the ball, to dribble it to the corner of the court, stop, pivot to face the basket and pass to

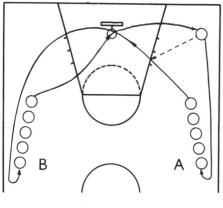

DIAGRAM 10

the cutter. Players move from file A to file B and from file B to file A. Diagram 10 illustrates this practice.

Three Lane Lay-up

This gives practice in taking the lay-up shot after cutting and receiving a pass from a team-mate stationed at the free-throw line.

The players are divided into three files. The ball starts in file A, is then passed to the front player in file B at the free throw line, and this player passes it to the cutter from C who goes in for the shot. After passing from file A, the player goes to the back of file B. After passing from file B to the cutter, the player moves in for the rebound, retrieves the ball and passes out to the player standing at the front of file A. Once the pass out is completed, the rebounder goes to the back of file C. The shooter, who cut from the front of file C, moves to the back of File A. This practice can be varied to have the cutter come from the left and this variation, because of the number of passes involved, is also a good passing practice.

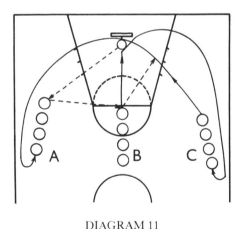

DIAGRAM 11

All the practices that have been described above can finish with a jump shot instead of a lay-up shot. In addition the player moving in for the rebound can, if the shot is missed, endeavour to tip the ball into the basket.

Tip-in Shot

If the coach wishes to give more emphasis to the tip-in shot, he should use the two file lay-up drill but ask the initial shooter to aim to miss the basket, by throwing the ball high on the backboard, so that the ball rebounds to give the player from the rebound file B an opportunity for a tip-in shot. The second player from file A moves in to retrieve the ball from the tip-in shot and passes to the next player in file B, who drives in for the next set up off the backboard. This is taken by the next player from team A, who attempts to tip-in the ball into the basket. Thus the tip-in shot is practised from one side and then the other. It is important that the player who is to practise the tip-in shot times his cut in so as to be able to take the feed set up by the player from the opposite file (diagram 12).

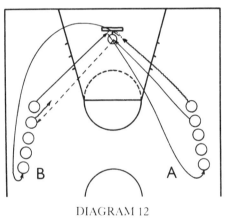

DIAGRAM 12

Twenty-one

The group is divided into two or four teams and one team is stationed at each end of the free throw lines, with players in a file one behind the other. The first player in each file has a ball and on the given signal he shoots. After taking the shot, he moves in to retrieve the ball or gain the rebound and then passes out to the next player in the file. After passing out, the player goes to the end of the file. Each player repeats the routine. The first team to score twenty-one is the winner.

A variation on this practice would be to implement the same procedure except that the player, if he does not score with the long shot, may move in to gather the rebound and take a short shot. No bounce or dribble is permitted; if the ball touches the floor no short shot can be taken and the ball is passed out to the next player. The successful long shot scores two points and the successful short shot one point.

Golf

The coach marks chalk numbers from one to nine on the floor. Starting at number one, each player shoots the ball and remains at this position until he scores. After scoring the player moves on to the next number. The player who completes the nine 'holes' in the fewest shots is the winner (diagram 13).

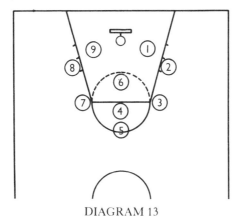

DIAGRAM 13

Jump Shot versus Opponent

Players work in pairs. One player with the ball, starting under the basket, passes it out to the shooter, who takes an immediate jump shot or moves laterally, using a one-bounce dribble to avoid the defender, and then takes the jump shot. The player under the basket, after passing out, moves out to defend. The shooter takes a set number of shots before changing his role with the defender. Twenty-five shots is the recommended number.

Percentage Shooting

Players work in pairs, with one player shooting and the other rebounding and feeding the ball out to the shooter. The shooter keeps count of the number of shots scored while the rebounder counts until twenty-five shots have been made. The players then change roles. Multiplying the number of scores by four gives the shooting percentage. Players should aim to score at least 30% of all the shots taken.

One versus One

The one versus one practice, in which one player has the ball and the other acts as a defender, is a basic offensive practice. It will give the players an opportunity to practise their shots against defensive pressure.

Free Throw Practice

This should involve two factors: fatigue and mental pressure. To create the fatigue factor the coach can at odd times during training make the players practise their free throws. As only two free throws are taken in the game at one time, this break can be fairly short — players just take it in turn to shoot two free throws. They are expected to score both! To create realistic mental pressure outside the game is difficult, but a technique that can be used is to name a player from the training group, just prior to the group carrying out some hard physical work, and if this player can score both free throws you halve the dose of physical work!

With any of these shooting practices that do not involve a defender, especially those taken close to the basket, the coach should be asking for a score on each shot. It is easy for the players to go through the mechanics of the practice but to miss scoring many shots. The coach should stress concentration on the scoring task. In the two file lay-up practice he could, for example, require all the players in the group to score consecutively. Until they have each scored consecutively, they keep on with the practice. This demands concentration.

✗ CATCHING

Catching the ball will be closely connected with passing, the speed and direction of the ball, the movements of the receiver and opponents, and what the receiver intends to do after reception of the ball. The actual technique of catching the ball is merely a means to another end and should never be considered an end in itself. Points in the technique used to catch the ball that should be covered are:

1. Anticipation of the receipt of the ball by signalling for the pass. The signal by the receiver not only tells the passer of the receiver's readiness to receive and where he wants the ball, but also prepares the receiver for the catch.

2. Concentration on the ball enables the receiver to ascertain the flight of the ball correctly — this is particularly important early in the pass. A potential receiver should be watching the ball even before it leaves the passer's hands and his tracking of the flight of the ball plays the most important part in successful catching.

3. Concentration on the ball enables the receiver to adjust his position so that he can get as near as possible to the line of flight.

4. Wherever possible two hands should be used for catching. When it is not possible to make the first contact on the ball with both hands, a one-hand initial contact is made but the ball should be brought under control in two hands as soon as possible.

Catching the ball should involve cushioning it with the fingers while keeping it off the palm of the hand. A basketball is played with the fingers — the whole length of the fingers, not the finger-tips or the palm of the hand.

5. The receiver should aim to move to meet the ball. This has two purposes; it enables an early contact to be made with the ball and it makes it difficult for an opponent to step in front of the receiver and gain an interception. This movement towards the ball can involve reaching out with the arms and/or actual movement by the receiver towards the ball.

6. Having made contact with the ball, the receiver should bring the ball under control. The hands should cushion the ball by relaxing the elbows and bringing the ball to a position in front of the upper part of the body ready for the next movement. This position, being a strong one, protects the ball.

7. To give the ball more protection, the closely marked player can, on catching the ball, turn his grip so that one hand is on top of the ball and the other underneath. This makes it difficult for an opponent to slap the ball away. However, it should be noted that the ball should not be drawn in close to the body as this will make it easier for an opponent to tie-up to the ball and gain a held ball call from the official.

8. Successful catching will depend a great deal on good passing. The accuracy and speed of the pass are particularly important. The receiver will find it easier to catch the ball if it is not spinning and not travelling too fast. The pass must be in sympathy with the receiver, bearing in mind the distance he is away from the passer, as well as the speed and direction in which he is travelling. The weaker player will need more room in which to catch the ball and space will give him time.

When catching from a rebound the player should aim to get his head under the ball, timing the jump to take the ball after it leaves the backboard and ring, and take the ball in two hands, bringing it down once possession is gained.

Teaching and Training

It is difficult completely to isolate the teaching of catching from the teaching of passing, so during the instructional phase of teaching passing the players should at some stage pay attention to catching. At this early stage with beginners a useful teaching point is to ask them to use their ears! If the ball is caught correctly, that is caught with an action in which the ball is grasped with the fingers, it will be fairly quiet, but if the ball slaps into the palm of the hands, then the ball has been caught incorrectly. With beginners other points to emphasize are: catch with two hands, go to meet the ball and get yourself behind the ball.

All the passing practices given earlier are also catching practices.

BODY CONTROL AND FOOTWORK

Good body balance is the basis of all individual skills in basketball. Although a player may be able on some occasions to perform when out of balance, these occasions will be limited. In this chapter on individual skills control has been stressed, and this control will depend upon sound body balance. The ability to be able to start quickly, stop, change pace, change direction and to perform the fundamental skills of the game depends upon the player being under control.

The basic basketball stance is one in which the player stands with feet spread, about shoulder width apart, one foot slightly ahead of the other, knees slightly bent, weight evenly distributed over the feet, and arms flexed and away from the body. The player should be in a slightly crouched position with slight flexing in the knees and hips. From this position the player is prepared to move off in any direction. His movement will depend upon efficient footwork. The balanced position with knees flexed lowers the centre of gravity and the spread of the feet widens the base and gives more equilibrium. To start quickly the player must upset this equilibrium. The sprint start position adopted by athletes is unsuitable for basketball, but the principle that the feet of the sprinter are outside the vertical line connecting the player's centre of gravity to the ground is the same for the basketball player. To move off in a horizontal direction the player can either over-balance in the desired direction and then push off with his feet, or he can lower his weight and put one foot out in the opposite direction to that in which he wishes to travel and then push. The second method is more usual for the basketball player not only in starting but also in changing direction.

Footwork is important when the player stops. To be able to stop quickly the weight is again lowered, the feet spread and knees bent. The feet move out ahead of the centre of gravity so that they can act as a brake to the forward movement. Bending the knees lowers the centre of gravity and helps give stability. The basketball player has to learn to stop when he has the ball in his possession and in this situation his stopping is limited by the rules of the game.

A two-count rhythm is the basis of footwork with the ball. If the ball is caught with one foot on the floor (count one) this becomes the pivot foot and the other foot (count two) is the foot used in stepping in the pivot. The pivot foot having been established it cannot be changed, nor may the pivot foot be lifted and grounded again with the ball still in the player's possession. The player may lift the pivot foot when he shoots or when passing, provided that the ball leaves his hand before the pivot foot again touches the floor. However, when starting the dribble, a player must release the ball to start the dribble before the pivot foot leaves the ground. The player who has used a one-two count in coming to a stop will have taken the ball with both feet off the ground, or with one foot grounded, and will plant this lead foot firmly on the ground. He will then lower his weight and bring the other foot forward with a slightly longer stride. This is usually called a 'stride stop' Figure 9 shows a player using a stride stop to come to a stop with the ball. The player takes the ball in the air, lands first on the right foot, which becomes the pivot foot, and then puts the left foot down.

FIGURE 9

A player can choose to use a one-count rhythm, in which case the player takes the ball in the air and lands with two feet simultaneously. The player, taking the ball in the air, lands with both feet well spread and parallel, dropping the hips low and slightly back in a sitting-type action. This is referred to as a 'jump' or 'scoot' stop (figure 10). The jump stop has an advantage in that the player who has used this stop may select either foot as the pivot foot, whereas with the stride stop only the one-count foot may be used as the pivot foot.

Sound pivoting is important for the offensive players whc use the pivot to move their position legally without dribbling the ball. The pivot is also used to protect the ball and retain possession, to out-manoeuvre and work around an opponent, to manoeuvre through the front line of the defence, and to

FIGURE 10

work away from the side or out of a corner.

At an early stage in learning the game the player who has come to a stop with his back to the basket is taught to use a pivot to face the basket and the opponent. If closely guarded he may pivot away from an opponent to protect the ball or to manoeuvre as part of a fake. Pivots and turns should be practised using both right and left feet as the pivot foot and through the full 360°, so that the player learns to use the pivot to change from one direction to the opposite direction, thus using all the playing area.

Basketball players seldom move around the court at top speed; rather they move at a controlled speed. The player must be prepared to stop and change direction quickly — this he can only do if he is under control. The faster the player is moving on the court the more difficult he will find controlling the ball as he moves with it or receives it on the move. A natural running action is the basis of movement around the court in basketball rather than a series of hops, skips and jumps. A useful principle to apply is that the player when playing the game should always be able to accelerate under control and have control of the ball.

Teaching and Training

This should seldom be done in isolation from other skills. The danger of teaching footwork skills in isolation is that they become overlearnt as when a player is very good at pivoting, but uses it for no apparent reason. Initially the pivot should be taught to enable a passer to gain or regain balance, or to face in the direction of the team-mate to whom he wishes to pass.

The teacher may wish to give practice in stopping with the ball, i.e. practice in the stride stop and the jump stop. This can be done easily in pairs, with a ball for each pair. The player with the ball passes to the team-mate, who performs the appropriate stop. If the pass is made at a right angle to the direction of movement, this will make it easier for the player practising the stop.

At all times the teacher or coach should be concerned that his players are under control and on balance, for without these qualities the execution of other techniques becomes more difficult.

✗ DRIBBLE

Dribbling, when used correctly and at the right time in the game, plays a very important part in offensive basketball. It is the only method that a player can employ to move with the ball in his possession from one part of the court to another. Unfortunately dribbling has gained a bad name as an offensive weapon, due to the misuse of the skill by players who fail to appreciate that, although the dribble has an important part to play in team offence, it should not be used so often that it is to the detriment of the team's effort. The important main uses of the dribble are:

1. Using the dribble to penetrate the defence to obtain a close shot at the basket — the individual offensive drive is covered in detail later.
2. To advance the ball into the front court on offence.
3. To move the ball out of a congested area — frequently used after gaining a rebound.
4. To retain possession of the ball as part of a stall.
5. To create passing lanes on offence. Usually this will be a one lane dribble.

6. To prevent a travelling violation when taking the ball on the move.

Dribbling can be misused if, for example, the player dribbles when it would be better to pass. However, this does not alter the importance of the skill and players should be encouraged to develop a high level of proficiency in dribbling.

Dribbling, like passing and shooting, involves the use of wrist and fingers to control the ball. The fingers are used to push the ball towards the floor, with the wrist and arm being used to control the height and speed of the bounce. The dribbling hand should be on top of the ball. Players should aim to be able to dribble equally well with both hands. To be able to maintain adequate control of the ball the dribbler needs to bend his knees and flex slightly at the hips, so that he takes up a protective crouch around the bouncing ball. The degree of crouch will vary according to the situation: if the player is driving past an opponent in a move towards the basket he will not be as low as if he were being closely marked or were moving the ball from a congested area. The dribbler uses his body as a shield to protect the bouncing ball from an opponent by keeping his body between the opponent and the ball.

Obviously the dribbler will not be able to protect the ball adequately if he is unable to see where the opponent is stationed. This is one reason why it is essential that a player can dribble the ball without looking at it. A good player dribbles the ball using the sense of touch — he does not consciously look at the ball, although it may be within his peripheral vision. Ability to dribble without looking at the ball will enable the offensive player not only to have the capacity to avoid opponents but also to see team-mates and thus be able to see the offensive opportunities that are occurring. The player who can dribble effectively with both hands will be able to change hands when closely marked and so maintain the protective shield he gains from dribbling the ball on the side of his body away from the defender. The dribbler will need to be able to change hands, change direction, change pace and also change the rhythm of the dribble (i.e. to vary the height of the bounce) to be able to take advantage of individual offensive opportunities.

The dribble should not become an end in itself but a link with other skills, particularly shooting and passing.

When starting the dribble against a defender, the dribbler is required by the rules to release the ball at the start of the dribble prior to lifting the pivot foot from the ground. A good offensive stance with knees bent, feet spread, with one foot in advance of the other, will help prevent breaking this rule.

Teaching

When teaching dribbling the teacher should be concerned firstly with understanding and secondly with familiarity with the bouncing ball.

1. Understanding is particularly concerned with when to dribble. With beginners this will be the use of the dribble to take the ball past an opponent to the basket.
2. Familiarity with the bouncing ball and what the player can do while the ball is bouncing. A useful practice for this would be to give each player a ball and for them to commence bouncing the ball. What can a player do while he is bouncing the ball?

(a) *Change hands:* This is vital in basketball. Although with beginners we would not recommend that they develop the ability to shoot with both hands, they must be able to dribble with both hands.

(b) *Change direction:* There should be sharp changes of direction — no smooth curves. Most basketball courts have a series of lines on them which can be employed to help the player make the sharp change of direction — right-angle change of direction and the change from going in one direction to going back the way the player has just come. The teacher could ask his players to change hands on each change of direction and to keep the ball on that hand until the next change of direction occurs. This will help the players develop the ability to use both hands.

(c) *Change of speed:* By this is meant the variation in speed of movement of the player with the ball. The teacher will therefore want his players to change from slow to fast movement and back to slow again. In basketball a useful method of beating an opponent is to dribble towards the basket, to stop, or almost stop, the forward movement, but keep the dribble going and then sprint past the opponent as he closes up to the dribbler. Thus the movement is towards the basket, a pause and then a sprint past, keeping the dribble going throughout.

(*d*) *Change of height:* The player will make changes in the height of the bounce of the ball fairly naturally. The low bounce of the dribble, below waist or even knee level, enables the dribbler to gain more control of the ball for the other changes and helps protect the ball from an opponent.

(*e*) *Change of position of the bouncing ball relative to the dribbler:* This includes dribbling behind the back and between the legs while moving forward. The player may also vary his position relative to the ball by dribbling the ball in one direction, pivoting, changing hands and moving in a new direction. This type of manoeuvre leads on to the Reverse Dribble mentioned on page 72 and illustrated in figure 12

Having worked alone with the ball the player should then work against an opponent to develop the ability to shield the ball. This is a free one versus one practice without direction. To make the practice more realistic the dribbler should be required to take the ball past the opponent to a target, which can initially be large, for example to dribble the ball from one side of the gymnasium to touch the wall at the other side. As the players increase in skill the target should become limited to the basketball target.

Training

Although it is possible to find practices of dribbling listed in books, for example dribble relays or dribble relays round chairs, the best dribble practice is one versus one. One player has the ball and the other is the defender endeavouring to stop his opponent scoring a basket. The ball handler uses the dribble to beat his opponent. Variation should be made in the starting distance from the goal, which could be from 18 feet from the basket, or from one end of the court, to take the ball in to score at the opposite end. All the time the defender endeavours to prevent the score.

INDIVIDUAL SKILLS — OFFENCE AND DEFENCE

INDIVIDUAL OFFENCE WITH THE BALL

The player with the ball has four options open to him:
1. Take a shot.
2. Dribble with the ball.
3. Pass to a team-mate.
4. Hold the ball.

Before he uses one of these options, he may fake, but his choice is influenced by the opposition and by his own team-mates' actions.

Prior to receiving the ball the player may have been forced by a close-marking opponent to free himself to receive the pass. With the opponent marking between man and basket, this movement to receive the ball will frequently be away from the basket and the pass made so that the receiver takes it with his body between ball and defender. A player holding the ball and not facing the basket is not a direct scoring threat to the defenders unless he is close to the backboard. To threaten the opposition the player should pivot to face the basket once he has the ball under control. As the players develop in skill they will need to learn to hold their position and receive a pass, even though they are closely marked. In this situation the pass must be made to the side away from the defender so that the player can receive the ball with his body between his opponent and the reception point.

Against the man-to-man defence a player should always know who is marking him, as this knowledge will help him to decide whether or not he is free.

Protection of the ball

When receiving the ball when closely marked the offensive player must be prepared to take action to protect the ball. Initially this will involve two hands on the ball and, after the catch, bringing the ball close but not up to the body. This may still give insufficient protection, in which case a pivot to move away from the defender should be employed. The attacking player, when pivoting away, should always try to maintain his threatening position, facing the basket. This can best be achieved by the use of a pivot away from the opponent, so that the front foot becomes the pivot foot. Additional protection can be given by placing the ball so that the body shields the ball from the defender. In extreme cases a player may be forced to pivot so that he has his back to the basket and opponent; he has lost his quick shot option and is protecting the ball so well that he has done the job of the opponent and defended the basket! There is a place for this type of play, but not in the context of individual offence. The ball can be usefully protected by a player, particularly the taller player, holding it above forehead height. In this position the player has limited his offensive options because with the ball up he will be slower to start a dribble, as the distance the ball has to travel to the floor has increased. It is, however, a useful position for passing the ball over the head of a defender to a team-mates — particularly to the post player in the area under the basket, In protecting the ball, the offensive player should endeavour to maintain a position that threatens the opposition and in addition disguises his own intentions.

Basketball Stance

The player with the ball must be prepared to react quickly in most directions to a defender's mistakes or team-mate's movement. To do this the player must take up a stance that permits quick movement. The best stance is one with a lateral spread of the feet, about shoulder width apart, with one foot slightly ahead of the other, feet flat on the floor, weight evenly distributed, knees slightly bent and head up.

The Shot

The player's decision to shoot will take into account his ability and the position of his opponent. The ability to score from within the 18 foot range has been stressed and is again emphasised. If a player is a scoring threat from this range, he will force the defender to take up a position closer to the shooter. Players must be constantly on the look out for opportunities to shoot. The ability to select the right opportunity will only come if the coach, during training, includes practices which place the players in situations involving the presence of defenders who are making an effort to prevent the offensive player scoring. An important skill for a player to develop is his capacity to relate his own shooting ability to the position of defenders. The closer the defender is the more difficult it is to score consistently. Players should be discouraged from forcing shots when closely marked by a defender who is using his hands to break the shooter's concentration on the target. However, with inexperienced players the coach will find that they will frequently fail to take a shot, even when free within the 18 foot range of the basket — this may well be because they lack confidence. It is recommended that they are encouraged to shoot, so that they develop the ability to recognise when they are free. Making the decision when to shoot is important and the coach can give his players confidence by not being critical of the missed shot. The coach wants his players to be constantly looking for opportunities to shoot. The basic instruction to the player upon receiving a pass is to look at the basket — is the player in a position to shoot?

The Dribble

The dribble is used in the present offensive context to move the player who has the ball to a new position — usually closer to the basket for a high percentage scoring chance (shot). The rules limit the player to one dribble and the player who has the habit of bouncing the ball as soon as it has been received will become a liability to his team. Emphasis should be placed on teaching the players when to dribble and when not to. The offensive player with the ball should consider using the dribble to take the ball past a defender standing between him and the basket. In this one-versus-one situation the dribble past the opponent — the drive to give it the usual basketball term — is an important attacking weapon. What should the offensive player look for in this situation? He needs to be able to understand and interpret what is happening in front of him. In the one-versus-one situation what should the coach tell his players to look for? Firstly, the basket — can he shoot? Secondly, he should look for his opponent.

To help the reader understand the defender's role in enabling the offensive player to make the decision, we will conern ourselves with this, before looking at the dribble techniques that can be used.

Defensive Mistakes

The first question is, is the defender between the shooter and the basket? If *not*, the attacking player should drive for the basket. If the defender *is* there, the mistakes he may be making are those of balance relative to the shooter and the basket, or poor defensive stance.

1. Mistakes in balance relative to the opponent and the basket are:

(*a*) *Moving towards the attacking player.* This is the most commonly made mistake by a beginner who, after the man he is marking has received a pass, moves towards him. The defender, when moving forward, will find it difficult to change direction and move back to the basket. This mistake of the defender moving forward is one of the reasons that offensive players, upon receiving the ball (particularly when outside the key), should pivot, look at the basket and bring the ball to a position ready to shoot. The defender will be tempted to move forward to cover the shot, thus allowing the shooter to drive past him for the basket. This position ready to shoot should be with the ball held at chest level below the chin. From here the player can take the set shot and, if the defender does move forward, the offensive player does not have far to take the ball down to the floor for the dribble. In addition, the offensive player looks for defenders who over-balance forward, when they reach towards the ball in an effort to steal it.

(*b*) *Jumping up to check an anticipated shot.* While the defender is jumping up, the attacking player can go under and round him. Here again the attacker, looking for his shot, will find it possible to force the defender to commit himself.

(*c*) *Movement laterally — right or left.* If the defender moves off line, say the defensive movement is to the attacker's left, the dribble is made to the right and vice versa.

(*d*) *Moving backwards towards the basket.* This will usually be to cover a threatened dribble and gives the offensive player time for a shot.

To cause the defender to make these mistakes a fake may be necessary. If a fake is used that involves movement by the offensive player, it should not put the offensive player off balance — it is the defensive man who should be off balance.

FIGURE 11

2. Poor defensive stance.

If the defender takes up a poor defensive stance, the offensive player should be prepared to drive in to the basket. Mistakes in stance could be: legs straight, feet crossed, weight on the toes with heels off the ground, or a wide spread of the feet either sideways or backwards/forwards. The defender, with one foot well advanced, should be attacked with a drive down the side of the foot he has advanced.

Obviously, to be able to attack these mistakes the offensive player should be on balance, ready to move, with knees bent, and still have his dribble to come. Having gained an advantage of half a pace and having got head and shoulders past the defender, the driver should move direct to the basket and not take a circuitous route to score, as this would give the defender time to recover his defensive position.

This analysis of mistakes that a defender can make is a simplification, but these are the mistakes that the offensive player must learn to react to. He may find, in fact, that the defender fakes a movement to make the offensive player commit himself. The offensive player then finds himself starting his drive towards the basket, but the defender is still there. The driver may not charge into the defender as this is a foul, so a quick stop or change of direction will be necessary. The dribbler, however, having lost this phase of the 'duel', should try to keep the dribble going. If he is forced to stop his

FIGURE 11

dribble, he has lost one of his attacking options and will thus be easier to mark. There are a number of manoeuvres that a player can execute while dribbling the ball that can still give him the advantage in this one-versus-one situation.

Offensive Dribbling Manoeuvres

1. *Change of hands.* The change of hands as an offensive manoeuvre to beat an opponent is combined with a change of direction and is sometimes called a 'switch' dribble. This move is used when the defender is retreating with the dribbler but has moved over to the side of the dribbling hand. The dribbler switches the ball across in front of his body, keeping it close to him all the time. Little change of direction should be necessary, as the defender is now out of position and the dribbler should be able to step past the defender.

2. *Change of direction and change of hands.* The change of hands as an offensive manoeuvre may have to be combined with a change of direction to lose the defender. If the dribbler is dribbling with his right hand and wants to change direction to the left, he plants his right foot, drops his left shoulder and drives off hard to the left. The ball is changed from right to left hand as the right foot drives. The dribbling hand (the right) contacts the ball slightly at the side and it is angled across the body, with the dribble continued by the left hand. The change of direction is completed when the right foot steps across and past the defender. Figure 11 shows the offensive player using the change of hands and change of direction to beat the defender.

3. *Change of pace.* In this manoeuvre the dribbler, moving at a steady pace, beats the opponent by increasing his speed of movement. The dribbler can also obtain an advantage by slowing slightly to encourage the defender to move forward to close the gap and, as he does so, the dribbler increases his speed to give him the half pace advantage.

4. *Reverse dribble.* This is a useful manoeuvre when the defender is overplaying on the side of the dribbler to such an extent that the dribbler is likely to charge into the defender. If, for example, the dribbler is moving to his right and finds his movement blocked by the defender, he can lose the defender by stopping his movement momentarily with the left foot extended to keep his body between ball and the defender. The dribbler pivots on his left foot to put his back to the defender. The dribbling hand is now switched and a long step taken with the right foot past the defender. The dribble now continues with the left hand in the drive past the defender. Because the usual reaction of the defence to a reverse dribble is to retreat, the offensive player may use a series of reverses to move closer to the scoring area.

FIGURE 12

Fake

Basketball has sometimes been described as a game of faking. This is unfortunate and so often inexperienced players over-use the fake. The fake is used to deceive the opponent into misjudging what is about to happen. The opponent must be given time to 'fall for' the fake before another movement is made. Faking in offence should be linked with 'threatening' the basket. An offensive player who has received a pass, has pivoted to face the basket and is within the 10-20 feet range of the basket, has immediately threatened his opponent as soon as he looks in the direction of the basket. The mere act of looking at the basket may be sufficient to encourage a defender to jump to prevent the anticipated shot. There are numerous fakes that can be used: fake to shoot; fake to dribble right or left; fake to pass; fake with head, shoulder, feet or the ball. Obviously, linked with a shot, drive or pass, the number of combinations is considerable. In the one-versus-one situation with the ball some of the fakes have already been mentioned — these can include:

1. Faking the shot and, as the defender comes forward or jumps, the offensive player drives under and past him for the basket. This is sometimes referred to as an 'up and under'.

2. Step fake to drive and, as the defender moves back to cover, the offensive player draws back as though to shoot. As the defender again moves forward to cover this shot, the offensive player drives past and in for the shot. This is usually called a 'rocker step'.

3. The offensive player with the ball can make a short step — say to the right — as though to dribble in that direction, and, as the defender moves over to cover the drive, the offensive player again steps with the right foot only in the opposite direction. He then dribbles past the defender and in to the basket to the left. This is a 'step fake and drive'.

In all these one-versus-one offensive moves with the ball it is assumed that team-mates co-operate in the manoeuvre by clearing space and keeping other defenders occupied. This may be a false assumption when the game is played. The offensive player in the one-versus-one situation with the ball must be prepared to make a quick stop and pass, or, instead of taking a lay-up shot close to the basket, to take a jump shot. In the later chapter on team play (chapter 4) there will be further discussion of this point.

Teaching and Training

One of the most frequently used practices in basketball is the one-versus-one game. In this training game one player with the ball is marked by one opponent. The player with the ball, starting from a position 15-21 feet from the basket, endeavours to beat the defender and score. This he will do with a direct shot or from a drive to a new position for a shot.

In the early stages of teaching the one-versus-one game the players can be paired off, according to height, speed and ability, and allowed to play.

One versus One

There are three main ways of playing the one-versus-one game:

1. The players can change their attacking/defending roles after each attack.

2. The players toss to decide who starts first. The winner takes the attacking role and continues to attack as long as he continues to score or retain possession after a rebound. Should he lose possession, then the defender becomes the attacker. The attacking player starts each attack from a specified position, for example the top of the 'D'.

3. One player makes a set number of attacks, while the other player defends. Then they swop roles. The winner is the player who scores most baskets from the set number of attacks.

When teaching the individual offensive skills with the ball, the teacher may make the player with the ball practise a specific move, which the defender allows through by making the appropriate mistake for the offensive player to respond to or by being passive. Some practices and teaching points are given below that can be used to help players develop their offensive play with the ball.

(*a*) Straight drive past the opponent.
Working in threes, one player (the defender) stands stationary at the free throw line and the player with the ball drives straight past the defender for the basket. After the drive, the defender becomes the waiting player. The driver retrieves the ball and passes out to the third player, and then becomes the passive defender (diagram 14).

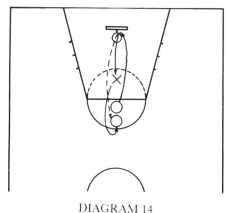

DIAGRAM 14

(*b*) Drive past the opponent who has stepped forward.
The practice is the same as for the straight drive (a), except that the defender steps towards the ball-handler before the drive is made. The drive should be started as the defender moves forward.

(*c*) Up and Under.
In this practice the offensive player fakes the shot and, as the

defender jumps to block the shot, the drive is made 'under' the defender. The coach, in addition to checking the general points made below, should check that the fake shot does not involve excessive movement — it should look like the start of a shot. In the game, just looking at the basket can be a sufficient fake. If you add to this a shrug of the shoulders and a slight lifting of the ball (say 6 inches), it will be sufficient to make many defenders respond.

(*d*) Foot fake and drive.

In this practice the defender is again required to make the appropriate mistake. The foot fake and drive, with a drive to the right, is used to make the defender move laterally to the left of the offensive player with the ball. This offensive player, with the right foot as the pivot foot, makes a short 'jab' step to the left with the left foot and at the same time moves the ball slightly in this direction. As the defender shifts his weight to the left, the offensive player steps again with the left foot to the right of the defender, so as to protect the ball on the drive. This left foot should step past the defender. For the foot fake and drive to the left of the defender, the left foot is the pivot foot and the steps are made with the right foot.

(*e*) Ball and head fake followed by a drive.

There is another practice in which the defender will initially be asked to move with the fake. This movement can be used when the pivot foot is inappropriate for the foot fake as described above. For example, if the player has established the left foot as the pivot foot and wants to drive to the right, this may be because the left-hand side of court is congested. The offensive player in this situation wants the defender to move laterally to the left but, if he was to step with his right foot to the left, he would place himself in a poor position to start a drive to the right. The offensive player in this situation can use a ball and head fake to the left to encourage the defender to think that he is about to dribble in that direction, and, as the defender moves, he can drive to the right. The movement described makes the protection of the ball more difficult, as it is the right leg that steps past the defender at the start of the right-hand dribble.

(*f*) Change direction on the dribble.

Practice of this will develop from the teaching of dribbling. Creating the appropriate position for the dribbler to execute the move will require the defender to overplay on the side of the dribbling hand. He thus leaves the other side open and creates a situation in which the change of direction would be used by the dribbler.

(*g*) The reverse dribble.
This will be practised in a similar way to the change of direction. Initially the players can practise this movement by slowly stepping towards the opponent with one foot, pivoting on this foot and turning the back on the opponent, and then stepping hard past the defender, with the non-pivot foot towards the basket. While this footwork is being carried out, the hand used to dribble the ball is changed. The coach should make his players practise the reverse from the right and from the left.

In these one-versus-one teaching and training practices the teacher should check that:

1. The start of the dribble is within the rules — that is, the pivot foot is not lifted until the ball has been released.
2. The drive step is hard past and close to the defender. The driver should drive his head and shoulders past the defender early in the movement.
3. The player, prior to starting the drive, has taken a stance that will facilitate a quick start — that is, knees bent with one foot ahead of the other.
4. The ball is protected by the body on the dribble, using the right hand when going to the right and using the left hand when going to the left.
5. The drive is made straight to the basket after going past the defender.
6. When practising, the players do not show a bias to their dominant hand in their driving. They must drive equally well to the right and to the left of the defender.
7. When working against a defender, the offensive player with the ball times the movement correctly, so that he initiates his movement when the defender is off balance.

Although these practices will give the players some confidence in the execution of the techniques, the most important skill in the one-versus-one situation is the recognition by the player with the ball of the mistake that is being made by the defensive player. After practice with a passive defence, the one-versus-one game with the defender active must be included. The teacher and the coach have an important role in pointing out to the offensive player the mistakes the defender has made or is making. The player has to recognise the situation and make the decision himself. The coach helps him to 'open his eyes'. The decision-making aspect is so important that beginners should play one-versus-one games early in their learning. At this early stage the teacher will in particular want them to recognise when the defender steps forward towards them — a mistake often made by beginner defenders. The 'bounce — one — two' used in teaching a lay-up shot is used in this situation.

A useful teaching aid to help the offensive player understand defensive errors is to make the defender stand astride a large cross, with the basket and the offensive player with the ball at opposite ends of one line of the cross. The teacher should point out to the learner that for the defender to move along any of the arms of the cross is a potential mistake that the offensive player can attack. For the defender to move forward is wrong — it allows the drive. For the defender to move backwards is wrong — it allows the shot. For the defender to move laterally to the right is wrong — it allows the drive to the left. For the defender to move laterally to the left is wrong — it allows the drive to the right. Even if the defender jumps up from the centre of the cross this is wrong — it allows the drive. All these mistakes can be attacked provided the offensive player has the necessary weapons (a right- and left-hand dribble, a jump shot, a lay-up shot and a set shot from 15-21 feet range) and the offensive player has taken a stance from which he can move quickly. If he has the weapons, all the offensive player needs is the ability to make the correct decision and respond to the defensive error.

INDIVIDUAL OFFENCE WITHOUT THE BALL

With only one player being able to have the ball in his possession at any one time, a player is likely, in theory, to play at least eighty per cent of the game without the ball. Play without the ball should be considered the most important aspect of the game on offence.

Moving Free to Receive a Pass

In order to get free to receive a pass a player will make one or a combination of the following movements:

1. Move towards the ball.
2. Move away from the ball and then move back to receive the ball in the space created by the movement away from the ball.
3. Move towards the basket and then go back out to receive the ball.
4. Use a change of direction and change of speed — in particular changing speed from slow to fast (walking to running).

When in the offensive area, a player must learn to get free to receive the pass so that, when he receives the ball, he is in a position to threaten to shoot, drive or pass to a team-mate near to the basket. It is comparatively easy, except against a pressing defence, to move free to receive a pass, but to receive the pass when one of the offensive options has been lost is more difficult. For example, the player moving free to receive the ball may move well outside a good percentage scoring area. Players need to be able to free themselves and receive the ball within a good percentage shooting area, or at least the area where the defender will be tempted to commit himself because he thinks the players may shoot. A simple way to get free is by the use of changes of direction and/or speed. Against a defender marking between the offensive player and the basket, a way to move free is for the offensive player to step towards the basket, then change direction and come back out to receive the pass. If this change of direction is combined with a change of speed, by the player walking towards the basket and then running out to receive the pass, it becomes easier to lose the defender. Figure 13 shows an offensive player using this method of moving free to receive a pass.

FIGURE 13

The distance that the offensive player will have to move in order to lose the defender will depend upon a number of factors: the ability of the defender; the defender's distance from the basket; and the position of the defender relative to the ball and the ball-handler. Remember that in the section on passing in chapter 2, stress was laid on the 15 feet passing range as the distance that enables quick passes to be made. The potential receiver should remember that by moving free he is aiming to create a passing lane for his team-mate with the ball. The player moving free and his team-mate with the ball must synchronise their movements and the pass, so that the ball is received before the defender has had time to recover. This may mean that the potential receiver will have to delay his move until the passer has the ball under control and is ready to pass. Too often a player moves free when his team-mate is still dribbling the ball or when he cannot see the potential receiver who is moving free. With the less expert passer more problems will be created if a number of team-mates are moving free at the same time. He can only make a decision to pass to one team-mate at any one moment in time. When he has made a decision about one team-mate, he can turn his attention to another.

It has been mentioned earlier that the ball should be received in a position so that the offensive player is a threat to the defenders. Obviously the further the player is away from the basket when he receives the ball, the less threat he will be to the defence. With the potential shot being the greatest threat to the defender, the ball should, if possible, be received at a distance from the basket where the attacking player can

FIGURE 13

threaten to score. Thus we have two co-ordinates in receiving a pass: the player wants to receive the ball 10-15 feet away from the team-mate and at a threatening range to the basket — that is within 21 feet of the basket. Players should be reminded that, if they have moved to the basket and then away from it to receive the ball, they should, upon receiving the ball, pivot to face the basket. A useful maxim is that 'the player with the ball outside the restricted area should pivot to face the basket'.

Clearing Space for a Team-mate

A basic ingredient of team play in all games is the creation of space. The good passing range that has already been emphasised, of 10-15 feet, is a useful guide to player spacing in basketball. Obviously, as basketball involves movement of players and the ball, this spacing is not always possible. It will be seen later that some of the basic team plays on offence, which enable a player to move free for a shot, involve players converging. Why, then, is it necessary to create space? First, playing in the 10-15 feet range forces the defence to mark on a one-to-one basis, thus allowing the team-mate to move into an attacking position without being closely marked, and, when an offensive player does move free, it is more difficult for the defenders, who are spread out, to help out. So the next point to note is that this spacing prevents one defender marking two offensive players. Finally and most important, players spaced 10-15 feet apart on offence have space to execute driving and cutting, and the distance makes it difficult for defenders to cover for a team-mate who is beaten.

The player without the ball on offence should be alert to what is happening on court and will have to control his desire to move constantly to a position to receive a pass. The method of moving free to receive a pass recommended above, i.e. the player moving to the basket and moving back out to receive the ball, will mean that this player has created his own space under the basket, so that, when he receives the ball and drives past the defender, the area under the basket is free. A team-mate who moves into this under-basket area bringing another defender with him will not be welcomed by his driving team-mate. When a team-mate is driving for the basket or cutting for the basket to receive a pass, his team-mates help by keeping away from the area into which he is moving. A player without the ball should aim to keep his immediate opponent so occupied that the defender cannot help and give depth to the defence. Often in the game the best thing that the player without the ball can do is nothing. Doing nothing is often doing something for team-mates.

Moving to Receive a Return Pass

Having passed the ball to a team-mate, the offensive player must look for an opportunity to move to receive a return pass. As in the one-versus-one game with the ball, the offensive player without the ball will be looking for mistakes by his opponent — mistakes of being off balance or moving to the wrong position similar to those mentioned earlier. Occasionally a defender marking an offensive player who has just passed the ball will either look to see where the ball has gone or endeavour to intercept the pass. Both of these actions are potential errors, which the player without the ball must look for and, if made, should attack by cutting towards the basket, signalling and looking for the return pass. This two-man offensive move is usually called 'give and go' and will be used in building up a team offence. The defender who does not make one of these mistakes can still be beaten by the offensive player using a change of pace or change of direction. Two commonly used changes of direction techniques are the 'drop step' and the 'reverse' (sometimes called a 'roll'). The drop step is a term that describes the action of a straightforward change of direction, in which a player moves in one direction, to the left for example, steps out with the left foot and drives off hard to the right off this foot, bringing the right foot forward and to the right, cutting past the opponent.

FIGURE 14

The reverse or roll is similar to the dribble reverse. It involves a change of direction, for example, the player moves to his left, then stops and pivots so that the player turns his back on the opponent and moves back in a new direction. Figure 15 illustrates a player using a reverse to move free.

FIGURE 15

The player's movements to get free to receive the ball usually involve movement towards the basket or towards the ball. This movement, if it causes commitment by the defender, becomes a fake and the offensive player moves free in a new direction. Inexperienced players usually move too much, or endeavour to move free without using a change of speed.

Establishing a Position as a Screen or Post

A 'screen' or a 'post' are terms used to describe a legal position taken by a player that obstructs the movement of an opponent. A screen (a post is a form of screen) occurs when an offensive player attempts to prevent an opponent from reaching a desired position or from maintaining his defensive position. A screen aims to impede momentarily the progress of the defender and to allow an offensive player to move free for a possible unimpeded shot, a clear path to the basket, or a clear path to receive a pass. The offensive player forming the screen aims to take up a position so that he obstructs the path of a defensive player who is endeavouring to follow his correct defensive position between offensive opponent and the basket. When the obstruction is set across his path, the defender is forced to go round the screen. The change of direction involved and the check in the defender's movements give the offensive player an advantage of time and space that can lead to a scoring opportunity. This obstruction may be referred to as a 'legal position'. To be legal the player making the obstruction must be stationary and not move into the path of the defender, when the screen is being used. The offensive player, when he takes up a position in front or to the side of the defender, is usually referred to as 'setting a screen', a 'front' or 'rear screen', as the case may be. If the obstruction is set behind the defender, to be legal it must be set at least one metre from the defender. A player setting a screen behind a defender is usually referred to as a 'post'. This term dates from the early history of the game when basketball was played in basement gymnasia, with pillars on the playing area to hold up the roof. The offensive players found that, by moving so that their opponent ran into the pillar, they could get free. When the game moved to playing areas without posts, the players used a team-mate as the post and moved, either with the ball on the dribble or without the ball, in such a direction that they could run the defender into the stationary team-mate who acted as a post. A basic post situation is one in which the offensive player takes a position behind the defender (usually at least 7 feet behind) in line between the team-mate he is setting the post for and the basket they are attacking.

The player setting the screen can, according to the rules, face in any direction. If set against a defender who is moving, it should be set between one and two metres from the defender — the distance depending upon the speed of movement of the defender. Although the screen can face in any direction, to gain maximum advantage and create the largest obstruction the player should stand facing the defender who is being screened, so that, if the defender made any attempt to avoid the screen, he would hit the screening player in the middle of the chest.

Sometimes the player without the ball has to be prepared to change position to act as a screen or a post for a team-mate to use. This is a two-way understanding, as his team-mate must appreciate that the screen has been set and know how to use it correctly. An example of a situation where a screen could be set is when a dribbler is endeavouring to bring the ball down court against a close-marking defender. If a team-mate moves and takes up a position along the line that the dribbler will take as he moves down court, the dribbler can lose his opponent by 'running' him into the screen. The screening player should stand astride the line that the defender wants to take to maintain his defensive position. Figures 19 and 22 illustrate a screen and a post respectively.

Should a player set a screen but find that his team-mate does not recognise the situation and use it, the screening player should not hold his position too long, as a screen involves the offensive players converging and, should the screen remain when he has not been used, he is liable to cause congestion on court. Players on offence endeavour to create space between themselves and team-mates — a divergent situation.

Using a Team-mate as a Screen

Obviously, if a player without the ball can create a screen

situation for a team-mate to use, the ball handler must be prepared to make use of a potential screen situation created by a team-mate. This naturally applies too to the screen and post situations mentioned above. These are not the only screen situations that occur in a game; others are less obvious. A common situation that can be used as a screen is where a player, who has dribbled but been forced to stop, pivots away from the defender in order to protect the ball. This player can be used as a screen by a team-mate who cuts close to the halted dribbler in such a way that the defender marking the cutter has to check his movements to avoid the player who has been forced to stop his dribble. The offensive player passes the ball to the cutter. This type of move is referred to as a 'brush-off screen'. A basketball coaching saying to describe this situation is: 'when the dribbler's forward progress is blocked, he should stop, pivot and pass to the cutter'.

It is vital that a player who is to use a screen waits for the screen to be established. The offensive player with the ball needs to be alert to the position of the screen and to the direction he must move in order to run his opponent into the screen. The offensive player using the screen endeavours to force his opponent to go over the piece of floor occupied by the screening player.

Manoeuvre to Gain a Rebound

The player without the ball must be alert and prepared to move in to obtain a position to gain an offensive rebound. This, of course, will depend upon the player learning to recognise when team-mates are about to shoot. When the shot is made, the offensive player makes an effort to obtain the inside position, between the defensive players and the basket. To gain this good, inside position, 4-6 feet from the backboard, will require aggressive movement by the offensive player. Having gained the inside position, he should protect it by taking up a fairly wide stance, knees bent, eyes on the ball, so that he can time his jump and reach to tip the ball into the basket. If unable to tip the ball back into the basket, the player should be prepared to grab the ball, come down to the floor and then immediately go back up again aggressively for a shot. If, when he comes down, he finds he is very closel·

marked and unable to shoot, he should move the ball from the congested area with a pass or dribble.

Change of Possession

The change of possession from defence to offence is a situation that the player without the ball must be prepared for. He should be prepared to move to take a pass from a team-mate who gained the defensive rebound or has stolen the ball. If, on obtaining possession of the ball, the team is fast breaking out of defence, the player without the ball must be alert to fill any free lanes.

Special Situations

On out-of-bounds, jump balls and in free throw situations, the player without the ball must be alert to carry out any duties required in any set play that his team may execute.

Teaching and Training

In teaching and developing the various skills involved in individual offence without the ball experience shows that most practices will require the presence of the opposition. It is, however, possible for players to practise the footwork involved in the changes of direction (the drop step and the reverse) without a defence, and the teacher may feel that this has some value in introducing the movements to his players. Players can practise these two footwork techniques at odd times, even walking down the street, by doing a 'drop step' to avoid somebody coming towards them, or the 'reverse' round a lamp post.

Getting Free to Receive a Pass

The serious work on individual offence without the ball will involve creating situations with defenders present. Diagram 8 illustrates a practice that can be used to improve scoring, using a lay-up shot after a pass and cut. This same exercise can be developed to give practice in getting free to receive a pass. It is done again working in threes, only this time the offensive player, who is ahead of the ball in the corner of the court, is marked on a one-to-one basis by the defender. This defender endeavours to prevent the player in the corner receiving a pass. The marked offensive player uses a move towards the basket and a break back out to receive the pass. The pass having been made to the corner, the passer cuts towards the basket, looking for a return pass. This player, having passed but prior to cutting, can execute a change of direction, even though he has no defender to beat. This change of direction is shown in diagram 15.

If the defender in this practice overplays the corner, then the offensive player in the corner should break to the area under the basket for the pass and, if he receives the pass in this area, he may shoot. The three players can take turns in this practice, if they rotate after a turn from cutter to defender and from defender to corner player, with the corner player moving out to take the ball and start the next turn of passing and cutting. Diagram 15 illustrates this practice.

DIAGRAM 15

This type of practice of two-versus-one, with the defender marking the player who is practising getting free to receive the pass, can be carried out at other positions on the court. The teacher should check that the players endeavouring to move free do not move too much. The movement to get free should be short and crisp. Too often inexperienced players run from one spot to another. If they keep attempting to run, they will find that they will have problems in losing their opponents, because, when running and changing direction, it will be necessary to slow down. This is a clue to the defender, so it is better to walk and then run.

Establishing a Post

Establishng the post position and passing to a post player requires practice of the timing of the manoeuvre. The offensive team wants to prevent the defensive team from having an opportunity to put pressure on the pass to a post player. To make receiving a pass in the post relatively easy, a post player should move out towards the ball and receive the pass as he comes to a jump stop. This will make it extremely difficult for the defender marking the post player to pressure the pass. There are two passes that are frequently used to feed a post player; the overhead pass and the one-hand bounce pass. The players making passes in to the post player in practice should, therefore, use one of these passes, with the· overhead pass being used more frequently.

Practice in establishing the post, passing in to the post player, then cutting close to the post player for the return pass and moving in for the shot can be obtained by using three players as previously described. Initially, the practice can be done with no defender in position. Diagram 16 illustrates the practice. The player who is to pass into the post player takes the ball at a position at least 10 feet from the edge of the key. The post player starts under the basket and breaks out to receive the ball just outside the key. After passing, the player cuts in close to the post player for the return pass and the shot. After taking the shot, the player retrieves the ball and passes out to the waiting player. The post player joins the end of the waiting file. The player, after passing out from under the basket, after an initial step towards the basket, breaks out to receive the pass at the post position. The coach should check the points on timing mentioned earlier. The player coming to the post position should establish a position with his feet just outside the restricted area. A post position should be established approximately in line between the offensive player who is to run his man into the post and the basket. The players should also practise setting, and using a post that has been set, at different angles to the basket.

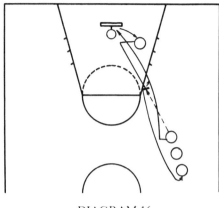

DIAGRAM 16

As the players improve the timing and passing in this situation, defenders can be introduced, but experience shows that the defenders need to be passive and allow the play to work. They can easily stop a straight pass and cut off the post manoeuvre, for example by the defender who is marking the post player stepping out and covering the cutter. This does not mean that the defenders would be able to stop a post play in the game situation, because the offensive players will have all their one-versus-one options open to them.

Establishing a Screen

The pick screen covered in chapter 5 is a side screeen and this again can be taught and practised using three players. To illustrate the appropriate position for the screen, the teacher should have one player, no. 1 in diagram 17, with the ball stand at the front and to the side of the key, with the opponent marking him stationed at one end of the free throw line. The offensive player should then attempt to drive to the right past the defender. The defender uses a sliding action with his feet, aiming to maintain his position between the driver and the basket. A check should be made of the floor that the defender moves over and, if possible, the path that he takes should be marked on the floor in chalk. Two offensive players should now take up guard positions, with the offensive player without the ball at the spot on the court from which the drive has just been started, and with the defender in the same position as previously. The guard passes the driver the ball and moves to stand with feet either side of the chalk line on the floor — this is the screen. Once the screen is set, the drive is made to the basket with the defender running in to the screen. The driver should face the basket after receiving the ball and could fake to dribble to the opposite side to that taken by the screen. This action by the offensive player with the ball gives time for the screen to be set. The screen should be facing the defender with feet shoulder-width apart, knees slightly bent, standing astride the line and within a metre of the defender. Diagram 17 illustrates this practice.

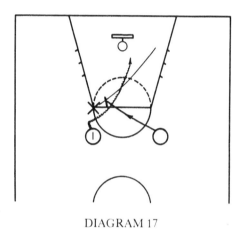

DIAGRAM 17

In the same way as was recommended with the post play practice and moving free to receive a pass, players should take it in turns to practise the setting of the screen and driving past the screen; and the screen should be set working from different positions on court and at different angles for the drive to the basket. When teaching screening, it is important that the players appreciate that the screen is stationed over the piece of floor that the defender *wants* to go over to maintain his defensive position.

Blocking out and Rebounding

When teaching and developing rebounding, the objective is to time the jump to take the ball at full stretch at the top of the jump. The players should be given practice in jumping to take the ball rebounding from the backboard. Initially this could be one player working alone, tossing the ball up onto the backboard, jumping and gathering the ball. Players could work in pairs, with one player tossing or shooting the ball on to the backboard for the rebounder. to jump and catch. This practice can be varied so that more than one player is a rebounder and the shooter aims to score. This gives a more realistic rebound situation. The group could be divided into two and placed in two files with the front man about 3 feet in front of the free throw line inside the key. The coach or another player shoots the ball to score. The first player in each line breaks in and endeavours to obtain the rebound; having gained the rebound, the player passes the ball back to the shooter and the two players who had moved in for the rebound go to the end of the files, and the practice is repeated. See diagram 18.

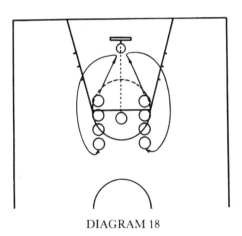

DIAGRAM 18

Rebound Timing

To help the players to develop the timing of their jumps another practice involving the players lining up in two files can be used. The two files line up on either side of the basket facing the backboard. The first player in each file tosses the ball up onto the backboard and moves out of the way, going to the end of the file. The second player in the file moves in for the rebound, taking the ball in the air and tapping it back on to the backboard. He also moves out to the back of the file, so that the third man can move in for the rebound, and the practice is repeated. The players in the file endeavour to keep the ball in the air. The coach could signal the next player to aim to tip the ball into the basket.

One-versus-one Blocking Out Practice

The players are paired off, with the player with the ball stationed under the backboard — his partner is at the free throw line. The ball is passed out, using a direct pass, and a shot is taken immediately. The player under the basket moves out and endeavours to block out the shooter and gain the rebound.

One-versus-one, Two-versus-two and Three-versus-three Games

All these practices provide opportunities for the coach to focus attention on the skill of blocking out.

INDIVIDUAL DEFENCE

The offensive team will endeavour to move the ball to a free player near to the basket so that he can take a shot with a high percentage chance of scoring. The primary objective for the defender is to prevent the opponent obtaining opportunities to take these easy, high percentage shots. You cannot stop an offensive player from shooting the ball, so the defensive effort should be directed to making the offensive team take shots they do not want to take — that is low percentage shots. These low percentage shots will be the long range shots and the closely marked shots pressured by the defender. The individual defensive effort should be concerned with limiting the options available to an offensive player that can lead to a score. These offensive options are the shot, drive, pass and move, either for the return pass or to screen. The defensive player should endeavour to reduce these individual offensive options. The defender should attempt to put pressure on possible shots and try to intercept drives, endeavouring to steer the driving player away from the basket or onto the driving player's weak dribbling hand. The defender should try to prevent passes to a player in the high percentage scoring area, and he should cover opponents' cuts and help team-mates on screen plays. The defender aims to prevent the opponent from doing what he wants to do by challenging every shot, every dribble, every pass, every movement of the opponent.

Before covering individual defence in some main game situations, a few basic points should be noted.

Position

The basic defensive position will be between the opponent and the basket. If the defender stands directly in line between the offensive player and the basket, the offensive player cannot take the most direct and quickest route to the basket. The offensive players may move freely around the court and this will necessitate the defensive players constantly adjusting their position. As the defender will always be second to know exactly what the offensive player is going to do, he will, by being between his opponent and the basket, have time to react to offensive moves. This slight advantage will be lost if the stance taken by the defender does not permit quick response and adjustment of position. This basic position between the opponent and the basket may be varied to cut out a particular option, for example a dribble to one side, and the distance that the defender stands from the offensive player will vary with the position on court and whether or not the opponent has the ball.

Defensive Stance

This should permit the defender to react quickly to offensive moves. The favoured stance is facing the opponent, with feet flat on the floor and spread about shoulder-width apart, with one foot slightly in advance of the other. The knees should be bent, seat down, hips slightly flexed and head up, so that the opponent can be seen. The eyes should be focused to the opponent's waist. Wherever the waist goes the rest of the offensive player will go — movement of the feet, the ball, the head or shoulders can be merely fakes. This stance gives a stance almost like a boxer's, except that the feet are not spread so far forward-backward. A rough guide on the distance of the spread of the feet would be that the toe of one foot will be approximately on a line with the heel of the other foot. It will be necessary to adjust the foot position according to the position of the opponent, the basket and the ball. The stance should give the defensive player a balanced position, permitting rapid movement in any direction.

Movement

The defender has to move in order to maintain his position in relation to his opponent, and his stance aims to make this movement possible. The offensive player may fake, change direction or stop quickly. All these moves the defender must be prepared for, and, if he has established a good stance initially, he should be able to accomplish this. A move by the defender can only be initiated if he is in contact with the floor. He should aim to keep his feet on the floor for as long as possible and, even when lifted, they should still be kept close to the floor. This will enable the defender to execute stops and changes of direction quickly. The defender, when following an opponent, endeavours to use a sliding action of the feet, and, by keeping his centre of gravity low by bending the knees, he will be able to make the quick changes of movement necessary to maintain a good defensive position. Figure 17 shows the defender using a sliding action of the feet to maintain his position. Although the defender should try not to cross his feet, he will sometimes have to change from the sliding action to a run, but even then the defender must be prepared to make changes of direction to follow the opponent. Good defence is played with the feet and the mind. The coach must require his players to bend their knees and use their feet to maintain their defensive position.

Arm Movements

The hands and arms can play an important part in defensive play. They can be used to help maintain balance and to bluff, bother, disconcert or distract offensive efforts to shoot, drive or pass. To maintain balance the hands and arms should be kept near to the body. In the stance referred to above the arms should be flexed, with the hands between thigh and shoulder height and the palms facing the opponent. If the defender thinks that the offensive player is about to shoot or pass, the hands can be lifted and moved so as to distract the offensive player. The defender will find that, if the arms are flexed at the elbow, he will be able to make faster movements with his hands. Care should be taken that the defender does not misuse his hands and arms, particularly when attempting to steal the ball. The defender's effort, when using his hands to go for the ball, should be to touch the ball rather than grab it. Touching the ball will make the offensive player move it away from the defender. If the defender is in the correct position, this will mean that the offensive player moves the ball from the most threatening position. Although he may attempt to steal the ball, the defender must avoid fouling or, as so often happens, commit himself and lose his balance. This loss of balance will often occur when the player, leading with his hands, lunges at the offensive player with the ball. It is better that the defender pressures the opponent, so as to make the offensive player concentrate on protecting the ball rather than on his offensive moves. Players should think of their hands as dissuaders — dissuade the opponent from shooting, dribbling close, or passing into the high percentage scoring area.

Mental Aspect of Defence

The defender must think and concentrate on what is happening during the game. This can be related to the options open to the offensive player — his reading of the play will be related to these options — which are the shot, the drive right or left, the pass, and the move to a new position. For example, the defender may find that the man he is marking can only dribble effectively with one hand and the opponent, therefore, moves in the same direction nearly every time — with the right-hand dribbler this will usually be to the defender's left.

Concentration on the opponent and thinking about what he can do are important elements in good defence. Each defender should work out how closely his own speed of reaction will allow him to move in to mark his offensive opponent. The defender should be constantly asking himself questions about the opponent he is marking: Can he shoot? Can he drive? Can

I stop or discourage his pass going into the high percentage scoring area? Is he a one-hand dribbler? What are his usual fakes? What is his job in the offensive team? Are most of his shots taken from one spot?, etc., etc. In addition to asking himself questions about the opponent he is marking, the defender should be considering what is happening around him: Where is the ball? What is happening to my team-mates? Do they need support? Am I alert to a screen being set by the offensive team? etc., etc. This constant questioning will enable the defender to anticipate offensive moves. He should be alert to cues that will tell him what is about to happen and this will demand concentration. Above all, good defensive play will depend upon the player taking a pride in his defensive ability and being prepared to work hard physically.

Communication on Defence

Thinking on defence and the ability to anticipate what is happening can be helped by communications received from defensive team-mates. Voice, therefore, plays an important part in team defence. This talking will include items that *inform* team-mates, for example the defender calling out the number of the player he is marking, and talking that *warns*, for example telling a team-mate when a screen is being set against him. The importance of using the voice on defence to develop team understanding and team morale should be emphasised by the coach.

Defence against an Opponent with the Ball

A number of points regarding defence against the opponent with the ball have already been made and others will be made when considering marking the dribbler and possible shooter. The way that the opponent with the ball is played defensively will depend upon the team defensive tactics being employed, so these comments should be read with this in mind. Thinking is obviously important so that the defender can anticipate possible moves. 'Can the opponent still use a dribble?' If he can, the defender should give himself a half-step 'cushion' away from the offensive player, so that he will have time to react to the possible drive. If the offensive opponent has used his dribble, the defender should be prepared to close the gap and swarm the opponent to make passing difficult. The amount of pressure placed on the offensive player will depend upon the team defensive tactics, but it is good play on defence for offensive players to know that they are being marked.

An offensive player who is about to shoot should not be allowed an unrestricted shot. The defender can discourage or distract the shooter by raising one or both hands. If the shooter is very close to the defender, the defender's hands should be above his head. Fouls on the shooter occur because of incorrect use of the hands by the defender. If the defender is going to attempt to deflect the shot, he should do it with an upward motion of the hand, rather than a smash down on the ball. Only tall players can expect to be able to check shots with a downward action without fouling. When marking a possible jump shot, the defender should not leave the floor too soon, particularly if the offensive player still has a dribble. A good guideline is: do not leave the floor until the offensive player leaves the floor.

Where possible, the defender should not give the opponent unrestricted movement about the court. The defender may not use contact to prevent an opponent from reaching a particular spot, but, if the defender can reach the point on the floor first, he may prevent an offensive player from occupying that spot, which may be the offensive player's favourite spot for shooting from. The defender should aim to cover the offensive player's direct route to the basket. The defender should realise that with a stance with one foot in advance of the other he will find he will be slightly slower in moving back on the side he has the foot forward. His rear foot should, therefore, be on the side of the opponent's direct route to basket, so that the defender can move fast in that direction. The majority of mistakes that defenders make when marking the player with the ball occur at the moment before the start of the dribble. Referring back to individual offences with the ball, it will be recalled that the offensive player was instructed to watch and attack errors of balance by the defender. The defender, when marking the player with the ball, endeavours to make none of these errors in balance. When the offensive player appears to be starting the dribble, the reaction of the defender should be to move slightly back, before moving into the path of the dribbler. This step back gives the defender time in which to move the correct way into the path of the dribble. Should the offensive player be faking, the defender, through dropping the foot back on the side of the fake, will only be allowing the offensive player the outside shot, but he will have covered the possible drive in for the closer shot.

To defend the shooter the player will look for clues that the shot is about to be taken. Has the offensive player a style of shooting which clearly indicates to the defender that a shot is about to be taken? The hand or hands are used, as in figure 16, to stop the shot. The defender, when attempting to defend the shot, should aim not to foul. Too often the defender, by waving his hands too much, fouls the shooter in a situation where the defender had already defended well and pressured the offensive player, so that the shot had become a low percentage shot.

FIGURE 16

Defence against the Dribbler

Mention has been made of the defender thinking about the dribbling hand of the opponent and of the opponent's usual fakes and favourite moves. Awareness of these points will help the defender when marking the dribbler. Playing against a right-handed dribbler, the defender could move his position so that he is no longer directly in line between the opponent and the basket, but is slightly off-line to the left (defender's left) of the direct line. In this position, with the defender having his left foot forward, the offensive player can be forced to go the long way round in his drive to the basket or to dribble with his left hand, neither of which the offensive player may wish or be able to do. In this way the initiative can pass from the offensive player to the defender. The defensive player against a dribbler must keep his feet moving and endeavour to maintain a lead on the dribbler. With skilful footwork the defender can direct the dribbler towards the side line away from the basket. When the offensive player with the ball starts to move, the defender's initial reaction should be to shift back slightly towards the basket away from the dribbler. Movement towards the dribbler can lead to fouling or falling for a fake. If the defender makes this initial step back, he can gain the leading position against the offensive player and stop the aggressive drive towards the basket. When marking the dribbler, the defender should keep his hands low, with the palms up. If an opportunity is presented for the defender to steal the ball because the dribbler fails to give the ball protection, the defender should concentrate on the ball and aim to deflect it with an upward movement of the hand. The defender should go for the deflection rather than the clear steal, because, if the defender goes for the clear steal, he is liable to commit the defensive foul that is so common and so unnecessary. Should the offensive player on the dribble move close to the basket in the key, then the defender should establish a firm position between the opponent and the basket, and not allow the dribbler to force him backwards towards the basket. The defender must be alert to the dribbler picking up the dribble — as soon as this occurs, the defender should close the gap and discourage the shot.

Against an inexperienced dribbler the defender, by faking a move to steal the ball, can cause the dribbler to pick it up. Against a dribbler who reverses, the defender should retreat. But, of course, as the dribbler moves closer to the basket, a stage will be reached where the retreating has to stop. The closer the offensive player is to the basket the closer he must be marked.

It is essential that defensive players protect the base line and do not allow a base line drive behind the backboard. A

base line drive is a potential danger to the defensive team
which, when it occurs, presents the defence with considerable
problems. The best defence is not to allow it to occur. The
defender marking an opponent attempting to drive the base
line should overplay the base line side of the dribbler, forcing
the latter to go inside where the defender can expect help from
team-mates.

Figure 17 shows a defender marking a dribbler. The
defender aims to make the only route for the dribbler to take
to the basket the one through the middle of the defender's
chest.

FIGURE 17

Defence against the Cutter

As the opponent who has been holding the ball passes, the
defender should step back to be ready for a possible cut by the
offensive player who is now without the ball. The step back
gives the defender time to cover a possible fake and cut. If the
offensive player starts to cut, the defender should aim to keep
ahead of the opponent, getting to the spot he is cutting to first,
overplaying the move and generally making the opponent go

where he does not want to. Defenders should be alert to pick up an open cutter who has beaten a defensive team-mate and moved into the high percentage scoring area for a pass. When marking a cutter, the defensive player should keep his arms up in an effort to discourage passes.

Defending an Opponent away from the Ball

When marking an opponent away from the ball, the defender will need to change his stance and basic position described earlier. The defender should alter his stance so that he can see both his opponent and the ball, moving slightly closer to the basket, away from the opponent. This step back towards the basket is called 'sagging'. When marking a player on the weak side, the defender will not only sag, but he will also move laterally across the court towards the ball — this is usually called 'floating'. If the ball is directly behind the defender, his first responsibility should be to watch and follow his opponent. He should make use of his peripheral vision with quick turns of the head to ascertain the position of the ball. Inexperienced players will find that pointing one hand slightly towards the opponent and the other hand towards the ball will help them in sighting the opponent and tracking the ball.

The defender marking the offensive player who has just passed the ball knows that his opponent cannot score — he has not got the ball — so the defender will sag to cover a possible cut for a 'give and go' type of move. The defender's sag should not be too far away from his opponent, because the opponent is still a potential pass receiver. The offensive player may receive an immediate return pass; should this happen and the defender is too far away from his opponent, this opponent may be able to take the outside shot, or to fake the shot and drive as the defender moves forward to mark him. The defender in this situation must keep alert and all defenders should aim to 'arrive' in their defensive position just before or as the ball is caught by the opponent. The defender can try to challenge the pass reception by the opponent. This will be achieved by the defender moving off-line and keeping close to the opponent, with one hand kept up, and in the most direct passing lane to the opponent. When the defender is thus overplaying the pass reception and the offensive player moves to basket to evade the defender, the defensive player should follow the offensive player, with arms up to prevent a lob pass being attempted.

Defence against the Post Player

When marking a player who is playing in the area of the key, the defender must appreciate that any player in this area is a possible scoring threat. Against a post player who has established a position close to basket, the defender may decide to alter his position so that he can prevent passes being made in to the opponent. Care will be necessary, as the position that the defender takes to prevent passes in should also enable him to react to moves made by the player in the post position. The closer the post player is to the basket the more care the defender should take in choosing a position to prevent pass reception. If the post player takes a position at the free throw line with his back to the basket, the defender should take a position behind him. As the post player moves down the side of the key, the defender should move slightly round him, so as to discourage any pass being made in to the post player. When the post player is playing low on the key, the defender should consider 'fronting' the post — that is taking a position between the post player and the ball. The defender, when marking a post player, should be close to the offensive player and have one hand touching him, so that, should this player move, the defender will be immediately aware of his movements and, if the movement is to basket, should follow the offensive player, with arms up, to dissuade any possible pass. The man marking the post player should tell his team-mates where the post is stationed, so that they can endeavour to prevent a pass being made by the offensive player they are marking in to the post player. Should the ball be passed in to the post player, then team-mates should be prepared to help pressure him and make his shot more difficult. The defender marking the post player should be concerned with preventing the highest percentage shot. That is, he will allow a jump shot rather than a lay-up shot. The great danger when marking a post player with the ball is that the defender will fall for a fake and leave the floor in an attempt to defend a shot, thus allowing the offensive player an even easier shot.

Defence against the Screen

Against opponents creating screens the defender who is being 'run into' the screen will be helped if the team-mate who is marking the player setting the screen gives a verbal warning to his fellow defender that the screen is *being* set. The defender, if marking a cutter using the screen, should use peripheral vision to see the screen and put one hand behind him, so that he can feel where the screen is stationed. The most important individual defensive aspect of defending a screen situation is the warnings given by the defender who is marking the player setting the screen. Further information on team tactics to combat the screen plays are given in chapter 5.

Pass Interception

The defender must remember that pass interception is a calculated risk. Should the interception be missed and the pass get through, the offensive player will usually be free to move in for a shot. Unless the passer is unskilled or the offensive team is making risky passes, interception of passes will require skilled play by the defenders. The defender should always watch carefully the style the opponents use in passing, particularly watching for any preliminary movements prior to release of the ball. Note if the player 'winds up' before the pass or stares at the potential receiver. Once the pass starts, the defender should concentrate on 'tracking' the early flight of the ball. All this information will help him to anticipate the flight path of the ball, so that he can move in to gain an interception. Long and cross-court passes are easier to intercept and, therefore, the defender should be prepared to take more chances on these types of pass. The defender can try to tempt the opponent into making what looks like a safe pass, for example a long pass down court, but, with careful positioning away from the potential receiver, the defender can give himself time and room in which to make the interception.

Rebounding and Blocking Out

An opportunity for a shot will depend initially on the team having possession of the ball. While the opponents have the ball, it is not possible to score, so players must be prepared to make every effort to gain possession of the ball in the 'free ball' situations. In every game the majority of free ball opportunities occur after a shot has been taken and missed. Both teams will be out to gain a new possession of the ball and this will depend upon their being able to gain an advantageous positon by 'blocking out' and 'rebounding'. These skills are the link between individual offence and individual defence.

Blocking out

This is gaining an advantageous position and occurs by establishing a position between the opponent and the backboard, when a shot has been taken. From this position a player should be able to jump and rebound the missed shot. The defender, who has maintained a position between his opponent and the basket, should, when the shot is taken, watch his opponent to see which way he is cutting in to obtain the rebound. The defender should then pivot into his path, so that the offensive player is faced with the defender's back. Communication between defenders can be important here, in that the defender marking the shooter can call 'shot', thus preparing his defensive team-mates to block out. Only when the defender has blocked out an opponent should he move in for the ball. In pivoting into the path of the cutter, the player must avoid fouling him. For example, if the offensive player is cutting to the defender's left, the defender should pivot on his left foot in a clockwise direction to face the backboard, so that he is between his opponent and the backboard and facing the backboard with his back to the offensive player. This movement of blocking out without committing a foul is illustrated in figure 18. If the offensive player tries to go round the defender, the defender should slide his feet to maintain the blocking out position between opponent and backboard. The further away opponents are blocked out from the basket the more space there is for the defenders to move in to take the rebound. The ideal blocking out situation for defenders would be for them to block out all offensive players at least 12 feet from the basket and then move in to collect the ball, which may be bouncing on the floor. This ideal is very unlikely ever to occur in a game of basketball and most blocking out occurs within the 10 feet range of the basket. Some teams make little effort to block out; instead all defenders move to the basket following a shot, thus congesting the area under the basket and making it extremely difficult for opponents to find any free spots. As the defenders should have the inside positon, this method of moving in for rebounds can be very successful.

Offensive players should not opt out of moving in for a rebound just because the defenders start with an advantage. They must be alert to defensive mistakes, such as turning to watch the ball too early or getting too far 'under' the backboard, and they should look for opportunities to cut unhindered to the area under the basket. The offensive player should, as soon as he or a team-mate has shot, make every effort to obtain the inside position, between the defender and the backboard. He should look for gaps in the area under the basket and cut aggressively for the inside position, about 4-6 feet away from the backboard. A player who has blocked out and obtained the inside position against an opponent should spread his stance to protect his position and make it more difficult for an opponent to reach the inside position. The player should have his knees bent and, if it is necessary to adjust his position because of movement by the opponent he has blocked out or because the ball is coming off the backboard in that particular direction, the player should slide his feet to the new position. Players should beware of obtaining a position too close to the backboard for the rebound, so that, when the ball rebounds, it goes over their heads to an opponent. The player who has blocked out should keep his arms down, with elbows slightly flexed, thus giving a position with the elbows above the hands. The palms of the hands should face back towards the opponent, so that they can be used to give extra information on the movement being made by the player who has been blocked out.

Rebounding

Having obtained the inside position, the player can now locate the ball and move towards it to gain the rebound. The players with the inside position will be aiming to time their jump so that they can jump up and slightly forward, lifting their arms up vigorously to grasp the ball in two hands. As soon as the rebounder has taken the ball, he should move to take it clear of other players, and this will usually mean bringing the ball

FIGURE 18

down. An offensive player may not aim to gain possession, instead he may endeavour to tip the ball back into the basket. Timing is critical, whether going for possession or the tip-in shot. Inexperienced players frequently jump too soon. To gain maximum height the player should start his jump from a wide stance, feet flat on the ground, knees bent and arms below shoulder height. From this position the player should jump vigorously, lifting his arms up and towards the ball. If the player who has gained possession is closely marked, he should shield the ball with his body. The offensive player, if he has gained possession, is likely to look for an opportunity to go straight back up for the shot. The defensive rebounder, having gained the ball, should look for a quick outlet pass to a team-mate, or use a dribble out from the crowded area under the basket to ensure protection from the steal or tie-up.

The holding the ball after gaining a rebound is important. The player who has gained the rebound will wish to protect the ball. If the player with the ball is tall, he should consider keeping the ball up and slightly in front of him. Too often the tall player, after gaining a rebound, brings the ball down to waist level and gives the smaller players a chance to tie up the ball. A smaller player, having obtained a rebound, should bring the ball down, but not close to the body. The hips should be flexed and the ball held in two hands, with the elbows flexed out, keeping the ball away from the body. The player who grasps the ball close to the body and wraps both arms and hands round the ball can neither pass nor dribble quickly, and is in danger of having an opponent place a hand on the ball, gaining a held ball decision from the referee.

Teaching and Training

Most of the practices that can be employed to help develop the individual defence ability of players have already been mentioned in the section on individual offence. Two of the most useful practices of individual defence are one-versus-one and two-versus-two, with the coaching instruction being given to the defensive players.

Footwork being such an important part of good individual defence, the players can be given some practices that focus attention on their footwork. The one-versus-one practice can be used, only the defender has to keep his hands behind his back. The offensive player endeavours to dribble past the defender who can only defend with a good position. If the attacker has to shoot the ball over the head of the defender, with the defender still between the offensive player and the basket, the defender is considered to have won this duel.

Another useful footwork practice, that can be used with the players working in pairs, is to have the player with the ball dribble up and down one side of a line on the court. The defender stays at the opposite side of the line and tries to follow the dribbler, who must make frequent changes of direction and speed, while working up and down the line. The dribbler should be working up and down a line about 15 feet long. This is a good dribbling practice, as well as a practice to make the defenders use their feet to stay with the opponent.

4

PRINCIPLES OF TEAM PLAY — OFFENCE AND DEFENCE

Each year in the United States a number of books on the game of basketball are published. These books, in addition to giving coverage of the individual skills of the game, set out the team tactics employed by the team that is coached by the author. Reading these various texts can give an impression that the game of basketball is exceedingly complex, with each team operating different tactics. However, careful study of these books reveals a number of common principles and in this chapter the intention is to set out the principles of team play from the offensive and defensive points of view.

In the opening chapter of this book stress was laid on the fact that offence and defence are inter-related and inter-dependent. Team tactics will depend upon the recognition and response to the opponent's defence or offence. Neither the offence nor the defence should be considered as distinct from each other, other than that possession of the ball will divide the offence from the defence phase of the game. The way the offensive team plays will depend upon the opponent's defensive tactics and vice versa. From a tactical point of view both teams will be endeavouring to dictate the way in which the game is played. Below a framework of the ingredients of defensive and offensive team play is set out. How each team puts these ingredients into practice in the game will depend upon their own abilities and the opponent's play.

POSSESSION

DEFENCE	OFFENCE
AIM	AIM

PRESSURE TO THE BALL — THREAT

mark the ball	threaten the basket
potential receivers	penetration
passing lanes	movement of the ball
depth	and/or a man

MATCHING OPPONENTS	USE OF SPACE

ability	support
floor formation	divergent and
	convergent situations

DEFENDING THE HIGH PERCENTAGE SCORING AREA — CREATING SCORING OPPORTUNITIES

Ball

prevent shot in the area

prevent pass into the area

prevent drive into the area

the player with the ball freeing himself

the player without the ball getting free to receive a pass

Man

prevent pass reception

prevent gaining rebound

prevent gaining position advantage

use of a screen situation

individual offensive options: shot, drive, pass, move

COMMUNICATION — ORGANISATION

IMPORTANCE OF INDIVIDUAL DEFENCE

TRANSPOSITION

DIAGRAM 19

TEAM DEFENCE

Aim

The defensive team will aim to gain possession of the ball without conceding a basket being scored against them. The defensive team can achieve this aim by preventing the opponents from taking shots that would have a high percentage chance of scoring. The defenders should encourage the low percentage shots and aim to gain the rebound from them. The low percentage shot is the long shot or the pressured shot — the latter is the shot taken by a player who is closely marked. The defenders can only very occasionally physically stop a shot without fouling, so their effort should be directed to discouraging shots, rather than attempting to block them.

The defensive team can gain possession of the ball through the interception of a pass, and pressing defensive tactics aim to cause the offensive team to throw a pass that is liable to be intercepted. Another way of gaining possession of the ball, without conceding a basket, is through the opponent's violation of the rules. With sound, close marking a defender could cause the offensive player to travel, double dribble or commit a charging foul. If the offensive players are lazy in their protection of the ball or can be forced into a situation where a closely marked offensive player is unable to release the ball within 5 seconds, then a defender can gain a held ball and, in the resulting jump ball, gain possession of it. The defenders have the opportunity of forcing a violation of the front to back court rule or the 10 seconds rule. These are the rules that state that the offensive team is required to move the ball into their front court within 10 seconds of gaining possession, and, having taken the ball into the front court, they are not permitted to take the ball back into the back court. Another rule which defenders may cause the opponents to break is that the ball has to be brought into play by the opponents from out-of-bounds within 5 seconds. With the defensive team having five players on court against the offensive team's four players, a chance could be created for a violation of the 5 seconds rule. As the rule requires that the offensive team must take a shot within 30 seconds of gaining possession, hard work by the defence that prevents the opponents moving the ball in for a close shot at the basket can lead to a violation of the rule. Alternatively the offensive team, by attempting not to break the rule, may be forced to take a hurried shot at the basket.

The defensive team may employ tactics which will enable them to conserve energy, by retreating and making their defensive movements on an inside arc close to the basket. The defenders may, of course, through playing a pressure type of defence, prevent an offensive team, who may lack fitness, from playing the game at a slow pace.

Defensive Pressure to the Ball

The ball, wherever it is on court, must be marked by the defensive team. This does not mean that the player with the ball should be closely marked — the defensive players may be sagging back to their own basket, but the ball is still marked. The player who has the ball in an offensive area must be marked in an effort to limit his offensive options in number and in strength. These options are to hold the ball, shoot, drive, or pass. To limit these options the defender may use the on-line principle, that is he can be stationed directly between his opponent and the basket; or he may employ the off-line principle, in which the defender takes up a position slightly to one side of the offensive player, although still between the opponent and the basket. The off-line principle is used in an effort to reduce the offensive option of a dribble to one side. The defender may also reduce the offensive options by pressing the opponent or by sagging. It may seem strange that the defender can use the opposites of the press or sag to cut offensive options, but these opposites limit different options. The press may be used to limit the shot or the pass — in particular the pass after the offensive player has used his dribble. Through sagging the defensive player, although giving away a shooting chance, may feel that this is a correct move due to the limited shooting ability of his opponent, and that by sagging he will be in a better position to cover the drive.

Potential pass receivers should be marked. How close they are marked will depend upon the team's defensive tactics. If the team is playing a pressure type of defence, then the potential pass receivers will be closely marked, and in this defence the defender may take a position between the opponent and the ball. If the team is not playing a pressure type of defence, then how closely the potential receivers are marked would depend upon the position of the offensive players and the distance they are from the basket. Each defensive player should know where the ball is and what is happening with the ball, because every time the ball is moved by the offensive team each defender must make some adjustment in his defensive position. If the defenders are alert to the ball, they can ensure more easily that passing lanes from the player with the ball are covered. The defenders can mark the passing lanes and discourage the offensive team from making use of certain passing lanes if they keep their arms up. The offensive player with the ball should see a forest of arms between him and the basket.

To counter the offensive team's attempts to create space, in particular space under the basket, the defensive team should try to give depth to their defence. They should play so that the offensive team have at least two defenders to beat before they can take a lay-up shot. Should an offensive player beat a defender on a drive or a cut, then the organisation of the defence should ensure that there is cover for any defender who is beaten. The offensive team will be attempting to create a numerical superiority — two-versus-one. The defensive team will try to achieve the same. Each defender should be confident that he will receive some support from team-mates when he is marking the player with the ball. The techniques employed to achieve this are sagging and floating. Sagging is the movement by a defender away from the man he is marking, back towards the basket. Floating is lateral movement made by a defender who is marking a player without the ball in which he moves laterally towards the ball; this move will occur particularly when the ball is on the opposite side of the court to the offensive player being marked. The defenders, when sagging or floating, must still be able to see their opponent and the further the opponent is away from the basket the further the defender can safely be from the offensive player he is marking. But defending players must remember that every movement of the ball on offence alters the situation and they may have to adjust their positions. Sagging and floating, when playing a man-to-man defensive team tactic or using a zone defence, aim to limit the room that the offensive team has to work in in the high percentage scoring area. Switching, a technique used to defend against a screen situation, results from defending the ball in depth. The defensive team should defend out from the basket. Most offensive teams want to penetrate the area under the basket with players and the ball. The defensive team should aim to keep this area covered by using sagging and floating techniques when playing man-to-man defence, or, if playing a zone defence, by ensuring that defenders do move towards the ball in response to its movements. The pressure towards the ball on defence, whether it be by marking potential pass receivers or through giving depth to the defence, should create a defensive situation where defensive players are able to support team-mates. The defensive player should consider channelling the offensive player's moves to where defensive team-mates are stationed. For example, a defender marking a post player can mark slightly to the side of the post where he will not be able to receive help from team-mates. With an offensive player playing in a low post position the defender will overplay slightly to the side of the base line, forcing the offensive player to go towards the middle, where the defender can expect to receive help from team-mates.

Matching Opponents

A team defensive play is very dependent upon the individual defensive ability of players. The team's defensive organisation will endeavour to match *offensive* ability with *defensive* ability. Slow players will be marking slow offensive players, tall players against tall players, fast players marked by fast defensive players. This is matching of talent. In addition the defensive team will try to match the offensive positional organisation of the opponents. If the offensive team plays using a 1:3:1 offensive formation, then the defenders should aim to match with this pattern. Matching the organisational pattern of the offensive team may create problems if the defenders are playing a zone defence. This has resulted in some coaches playing a sophisticated zone defence in which the defenders match the offensive formation but still play a zone defence. These sophisticated zone defences, which aim to match the offensive pattern, are for obvious reasons called 'match-up zones'.

Defending the High Percentage Scoring Area

This is priority and will need to be put into practice by all teams that are to have a successful team defence. Defending the high percentage scoring area can be considered under two headings: the ball and the man.

When defending the ball, the defensive team aims to prevent shots being taken in the danger area, prevent passes into this area and prevent opponents dribbling into the area. This will leave the offensive team with only low percentage shots. It is important to note that what may be a low percentage shot for one team may be a high percentage shot for another; what may be a high percentage shot for one player may be a low percentage scoring chance for another. A useful rule is that any shot taken within 18 feet from the basket is a high percentage shot, and a shot taken from the 18-25 feet range could, for some players, be a high percentage shot and should be marked if the opponent is scoring from this range. The defensive team cannot prevent an opponent from occupying a particular spot on the court, unless they can get to that spot first, so defending an opponent who has established a position or is moving to establish a position in the high percentage scoring area is important. Defence against this offensive player should be directed towards preventing him from receiving the ball.— a player without the ball cannot score. Defence should, therefore, prevent pass reception by marking passing lanes in to the player. This will involve not only the defender who is marking the player who has moved to the danger area, but also team-mates who are marking the offensive player with the ball. These team-mates can be helped by being told where the player who is in the danger area is stationed. The other way that the offensive team can gain possession of the ball in the high percentage scoring area is from a rebound. The defensive team must prevent the offensive players gaining the rebound by blocking them out and aggressively rebounding, so that the offensive team do not have a chance of a second shot. The defending team, in concentrating on depth in the defence, should not allow an opponent to obtain a position of advantage so that marking this player becomes difficult for a defender. It is important that offensive players moving in to the danger area should be marked and their movements covered by the defence. A defensive player must consider that an offensive player with the ball who has beaten another defender is his responsibility. This covering of the movement of offensive players can only be achieved if the defence is united as a team, and one way they can achieve this is by talking to each other.

Communication

Talking between defenders must be encouraged to enable the five defenders to be aware of the positions and movement of the offensive players. Defenders must communicate with each other. Who is marking the ball? Where are screens and posts being set? Where are the cutters moving to? What is the offensive formation behind the front members of the defence? This is information that will help the defence play as a team unit. Defenders must learn to communicate worthwhile information to team-mates.

Individual Defence

The importance of good, individual defensive ability cannot be over-emphasised. Without good, individual defensive ability any team defensive tactics are doomed to fail. Good defence requires the players to work hard and take pride in their defensive ability. The defender must look upon defending as a form of attack. The defender should aim to defend aggressively, to dominate the opponent and so force the offensive player to play defensively to protect his possession of the ball. The individual defensive skills are concerned with reducing the individual offensive options of the attacking players. Defence is the hard work phase of the game — players may rest slightly when on attack. Remember that good individual defence requires use of the feet and the mind.

TEAM OFFENCE

Aim

The aim of the offensive team is to turn each possession into a scored basket; they will not want to make a mistake that will lead to the loss of possession without taking a shot. The only occasion when a team may not attempt to turn a possession into a shot is towards the end of a half, when they may be attempting to waste time. A team will consume time when, late in the game, they wish to protect a small lead. The time during which they may retain possession without taking a shot is limited by the rules to 30 seconds. For example, a team with a lead of six points, with possession of the ball and one minute left to play, may make no effort to shoot, aiming rather to maintain possession of the ball for 30 seconds. Even if the opponents do score when they gain possession due to the 30 second violation, they cannot in theory win. The offensive team could be concerned with conserving energy by playing a slow tempo game or, through the use of a fast break, endeavour to tire their opponents.

Threat

When discussing basic offensive play, mention should be made of three points: the threatening of the basket by the offensive team; the penetration of the defence; and movement of man and/or the ball. These are linked but varying principles.

Threatening the basket

Each offensive player, when he receives the ball, should be prepared to threaten the basket, looking for opportunities to shoot, drive in for a closer shot or pass to a team-mate in the area under the basket. Thus, when moving free to receive a pass, the offensive player will, when in his front court, try to receive the ball at a point on the floor from which he can threaten to shoot. After receiving the pass, this may involve him pivoting so as to face the basket. The ease with which an offensive player pivots to face the basket will depend on how closely the defender is marking and on the footwork of the offensive player. With beginners and inexperienced players the teacher should make conditions for the game to prevent the opponents taking the ball from the offensive player and referee the game strictly with respect to the contact rules. If this is carried out, the offensive players will develop confidence in turning to threaten the basket.

Penetration

The greatest threat to the defence occurs when the ball penetrates to the high percentage scoring area. The closer the player with the ball is to the basket the more problems there are for the defensive team and the more response they will make to the situation. The ball may penetrate into this danger area for the defence on a drive or through a pass to an offensive player who has cut in to the area. The ball being in the area under the basket could well lead to the defensive team

DIAGRAM 20

having more than one player marking the offensive player with the ball, thus leaving an offensive player free. The 'base line drive', in which an offensive player drives along the base line to go behind the backboard, is a danger to the defenders and they are likely to over-protect and have more than one defender turn to mark the base line driver. These defenders now have their backs to other offensive players, who should try to cut to a free position in front of the basket in the centre of tne key. The offensive team will also need a player in the weak side forward position, that is facing the base line driver. Either of these offensive players could be free to receive a pass and take a shot. Diagram 20 illustrates these positions during the base line drive.

Although the offensive team may not be able to penetrate the area under the basket, the ball penetrating the front line of the defence will create problems for the defensive team. This penetration of the front line could be a pass into a player in the high post area or to a forward in the corner of the court.

Movement of the Ball and/or a Man

Penetration of the defence will involve movement of the ball and/or a player. Movement will present problems to the defence, who should react to each movement. The way in which the defence reacts to the movement could lead to a scoring chance being created. Movement by offensive players who are away from the ball will keep the defence occupied and discourage them from sagging or floating to give support to defensive team-mates. The offensive players should be prepared to pass the ball around. If the ball is held by one offensive player for too long, it allows the defence to get set. Movement of the ball, although of itself not necessarily freeing a player, can create a situation where a defender, by failing to respond correctly to the movement of the ball, allows an opportunity for the offensive player to create a scoring chance.

Movement will be necessary for the creation of scoring chances and the form that the movement takes will depend upon the defensive tactics. Against a defence that is basically man-to-man, emphasis should be on player movement, and against a zone defence emphasis should be on ball movement. Note that this is an emphasis. Player movement can help create scoring opportunities against a zone defence and ball movement can form a part of team offensive action against a man-to-man defence. Offensive teams frequently show a bias in their attacks, making more attacks down the right-hand side of the court than down the left. This should be avoided, as the defensive team will counter this and overplay the right-hand side of the court. A change of direction in the movement of the offence can create scoring chances: for example, if the ball is moved to the right-hand side of the court and the post player also moves to the right, the defenders will move in this direction to cover. A quick pass to the weak side could find a player free. Diagram 21 illustrates this move.

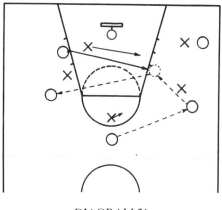

DIAGRAM 21

Use of Space

The offensive team will endeavour to establish space between players — the usual spacing being the 10-15 feet range, which is a good passing range. The offensive player with the ball should always have someone to pass to — this means that team-mates should be ready to create passing lanes. This support of the player with the ball should occur as soon as possession is gained. For example, a player who obtains a rebound at the defensive basket needs a team-mate to make the outlet pass to. This outlet pass will be easy if a team-mate moves to a support position, 10-15 feet away from the rebounder, at the side of the court. When the ball is out-of-bounds, team-mates of the player with the ball out-of-bounds need to move to receive the pass. However, the offensive team does not want all four players moving to receive the pass — some of the players on court will, rather than support the player with the ball, move to support team-mates who do not have the ball. Basketball being a quick passing game, this support of the player without the ball is important.

Spreading out creates space between the offensive players and this gives them room to execute scoring plays which are either individual drives or team plays involving cuts and screens. The offensive team will be endeavouring to create space in the area under the basket. The basic formations used by offensive teams, be it 2:1:2, 1:3:1 or 1:2:2, are ways in which the offensive team tries to dominate the defensive team by dictating where space will be. Which of the floor formations is used will depend upon individual abilities and upon the tactics employed by the defenders. For example, against a 2:1:2 zone defence, a usual offensive formation would be 1:3:1. It is usual that the formation used by the offensive team, and the offensive moves executed from these positions to create scoring chances, will be known to team players and will have been practised during training sessions. The spacing of the players should give a deployment so that there are offensive players on both sides of the court and at least one offensive player stationed in a safety position between the rest of the players on the court and the basket that the offensive team will have to defend when they lose possession of the ball. This player in the safety position will give some defensive cover, but more important, from the offensive point of view, this player will be in a position to receive a pass when the offensive players are in danger of losing the ball due to good defence or to offensive players getting in each other's way. The ball can be passed to the player in the safety position and a new attack started. This spacing of players is often referred to in basketball literature as 'offensive balance'.

Players in a particular formation should be assigned to rebounding roles and they should be prepared to move in to gain offensive rebounds, so that their team can have a second shot at the basket. The players assigned to this role will be the taller players, so their position in the formation will be near to the basket.

The movement of offensive players on court, when endeavouring to create scoring opportunities, will mean that players who may not be directly involved with the scoring player, other than to create space, will have to adjust their positions so as to maintain the offensive formation. Diagram 22 shows the type of movement that can occur when two players (numbers 1 and 2) execute a 'give and go' type of move. Player no. 2 passes the ball to player no. 1 and cuts for a return pass. If he does not receive the return pass, he should continue through and out to the other side of court. Player no. 1 with the ball now has no team-mate in the 10-15 feet range, so, to give this support, player no. 3 moves to the position on court formerly occupied by no. 2. Player no. 3 is replaced by no. 4, and the cutter (2) takes the place vacated by player no. 4. This movement is often referred to as a 'rotation play'. Players 1 and 5 will be the tallest players on the offensive team and do not join in the rotation, so that they remain in a good position to move in for the rebound. The original cutter (2) did the correct thing when he cut through and out the other side. This cut all the way through keeps the pressure on the defensive team and is preferable to an action in which the player cuts and, when he realises that he will not get the return pass, moves back out to his original position.

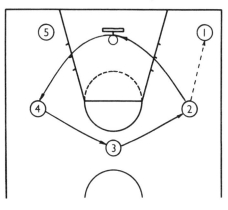

DIAGRAM 22

The offensive players, through this spacing, draw defenders away from each other and thereby create width for the offence. The offensive formation will give depth and create the 'man ahead' situation mentioned in chapter 1. On offence, the players should play at either the support range of 10-15 feet or close to a team-mate, as in a screen. This helps understanding. At the 10-15 feet range the players are easily available and looking to receive the pass, and both players can recognise this. When the offensive players converge on each other, they do this for a reason — to create a screen situation Playing at these two distinct ranges gives the offensive players information. When they move to a no-man's land, say 7-8 feet away from a team-mate, it is neither a clear screen nor a good passing range.

Creating Scoring Opportunities

The object of team co-operation is to free a player for a good shot, which is the shot that the player is confident he can take and from which he can score. Here we come back to the high percentage scoring area and the individual options open to an offensive player — shot, drive, pass and move. The particular options used, and deciding whether a fake will be necessary, depend upon the reaction of the defender to the offensive action. What will be a high percentage scoring shot for a player will vary from player to player, the position of the defender and the position on court. Within the game three basic methods of creating a scoring opportunity can be identified — these are:

(*a*)   The player with the ball freeing himself
(*b*)   A player without the ball getting free and receiving a pass
(*c*)   Through the use of a screen situation.

(*a*) *The player with the ball freeing himself.* Individual offence with the ball is covered in chapter 3. All that should be added at this stage is that the offensive player must be aware of what is happening with team-mates and other defenders. He must time his movements so that, if he is driving, the space he is heading for is still free and so that team-mates are ready to move in for possible rebounds should his shot miss.

(*b*) *A player without the ball getting free and receiving a pass.* This has been covered in chapter 3.

(*c*) *Through the use of a screen situation.* Some of the more common screen situations used in the game are covered in chapter 5. This convergence of players is counter to the principle of spacing. However, as players on the team will be endeavouring to maintain the balanced spacing of players, when two players on offence do converge, it will be a signal to the offensive players that a possible screen situation exists and will help the players be aware of what is happening in the game.

These basic methods of creating a scoring opportunity depend upon players being aware of the 'logic' of the game of basketball. This 'logic' could read as follows. Only the player with the ball can score; therefore, a player who has received the ball should look at the basket to see if he can take a scoring shot. If he finds he is not in a position to shoot, through being too far from the basket or being closely marked, then the second offensive option is that the player with the ball should look for the drive — that is to move towards the basket for a closer shot. If he can neither shoot nor drive, then he must pass. Having passed to a team-mate, the player should consider moving. The team-mate who has received the pass will be going through his own options of shooting or driving. When this new offensive player with the ball looks to see who he can pass to, the first player he should look for is for the player who gave him the ball, as this player could be moving, cutting for a return pass, or moving to set a screen either on the player with the ball or off the ball. The player who has passed the ball to the player with the ball should have the 'right' to move first. Assuming the players are spread out, the logic of the game gives this offensive routine to each individual player. This routine takes the player through his offensive options of shot, drive, pass or move. Before the player executes any of these options, he *may* fake; and which option he uses will depend upon the defensive play. These individual offensive options in logical order of execution are: SHOT, DRIVE, PASS (with the first option belonging to the man who passed to the player with the ball) and MOVE (to receive a return pass or to set a screen either on or away from the ball).

Organisation

Mention has been made of the use by the offensive team of particular floor formations. The basic floor formations used by the offensive team (2:1:2, 1:3:1 or 1:2:2) are ways in which that team tries to dominate the defensive team. From the basic floor formation the team will be able to make use of their individual players' abilities, thus ensuring, for example, that the best shooters are taking the shots and the best rebounders are in position to rebound. A team will have a number of pre-practised two- or three-man plays that they will use from their floor formation to create a scoring chance. The floor formation becomes a position of reference from which the attacking team challenges the defenders. The point of reference obtained by the organisation helps players to recognise what their team-mates are doing and their role in the total team attack. The rigidity with which the team uses the pre-practised moves varies from team to team. A completely free offence requires the players to have a clear understanding of the 'logic' of the game as mentioned above. The danger is that the organisation of moves will become too rigid. The individual player must be encouraged to look for his own offensive options. The offensive organisations should create situations that help the players recognise (*a*) mistakes made by the defenders, i.e. errors of individual defensive position, mistakes in stance and faults in the defensive pattern with reference to the offensive formation, and (*b*) the offensive manoeuvres being employed by team-mates. An offensive organisation that is too rigid can cause the offensive players to fail to recognise the defensive errors.

Transposition

The change from being the offensive team to becoming the defensive team at the loss of possession and vice versa is a critical stage in the game. The coach should be aiming for his team to respond instantly to this change. As the majority of changes of possession during a game occur after a shot, the rebounding of missed shots is important. The offensive team needs certain players to be responsible for moving in to gain a sound rebound position, while the rest of the defensive team tries to block-out the opposition, so that their team-mates can gain the rebound.

The change from offence to defence will involve controlling the opponent's fast break by marking the opponent who has gained possession. If this has occurred through a rebound, part of the defence should be to slow up the outlet pass by marking the rebounder closely and marking possible outlet pass receivers. A team will not only develop an *offensive* fast break, but also a *defensive* fast break. A quick return to defence, after having been on offence, will make it more difficult for the opposition to achieve numerical superiority through fast breaking. The new offensive team should, on gaining control of the ball, try to convert this possession into a shot before the defence has recovered and reorganised. This will involve a quick, controlled movement down court with the ball, aiming, through a fast offensive development, to advance the ball to the front court and into a scoring area before the defence is organised. If the team is to break fast successfully, players must respond instantly to the new possession, so that opportunities exist for the pass out from defence and, having made this first pass out, the player with the ball has support and is not expected to take on the opposition alone.

5

BASIC TEAM PLAY — OFFENCE AND DEFENCE

With five players on court, there are many offensive team manoeuvres that can be executed during the game to place the defence at a disadvantage and give an offensive player an opportunity for a shot. Obviously, the defence will influence the offensive manoeuvres by their position on court and distance from the basket. In this chapter some of the basic plays used during the game will be illustrated and a note made of the defensive tactics employed to counter the move. A team offence will be built on a one-versus-one, a two-versus-two and, occasionally, a three-versus-three situation. This chapter will be concerned mainly with two-versus-two situations. They are based upon two of the methods of creating a scoring situation — they are a player without the ball cutting free, and the use of a screen situation.

The one-versus-one situation with the ball has already been covered in some detail and, in all the play situations that follow, the reader should remember that the player with the ball always has the option of working alone to take advantage of an error by the man who is marking him.

Players on attack react to what action the defenders take, so it is important to give the defenders time to react, otherwise the offensive team will tend to overrun them before they have reacted to a play.

GIVE AND GO

This is a two-man offensive play in which one player passes to a team-mate and then cuts towards the basket, looking for a return pass.

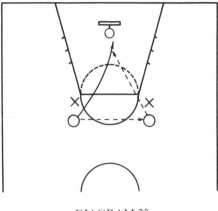

DIAGRAM 23

Offence

Diagram 23 illustrated the move being executed by two guards. The pass is made from the left to the right guard and the left guard (taking advantage of a momentary relaxation by his defender who, seeing the ball passed, thinks his job is finished) cuts into the space between the two defenders, gains the step advantage against the opponent, and takes the return pass as he moves to the basket. This guard-to-guard move is easier for the defensive team to cover, as the defender marking the potential cutter should be able to see both ball and man quite easily. If a 'give and go' is executed with the guard passing to a forward, the defender is likely to make the mistake of turning to see where the ball has gone or will move off the line in an effort to intercept the pass. If the defender does not make a mistake, the guard could use a move to the inside and then change direction, or he could reverse and cut for the return pass. The guard-to-forward 'give and go' will make it more difficult for the defenders not involved in the play to move over and help. The forward, when executing this play, can move free by taking his opponent to the basket, changing direction and moving out to the corner to receive the pass. The forward, on receiving the pass, should pivot to face the basket so that he has a clear view of his cutting team-mate. Providing the cutter is moving at an even speed, the forward should have no difficulty making the return pass, so that the shot can be taken on the run with no break in the action. Diagram 24 illustrates this 'give and go' worked between the guard and the forward.

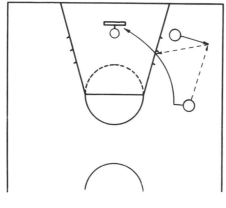

DIAGRAM 24

Defence

The defensive error is being made by the man marking the cutter and is made early in the cut. The defence against the 'give and go' is for the defender marking the player who passes and then cuts to sag immediately the opponent has released the pass. This gives the defender more time to follow the cut. The defensive team should be alert to a 'give and go' type of move to ensure that possible passes in to the cutting player are marked and that, through giving depth to the defence by sagging, the weak side defenders can help to mark the cutter.

BACKDOOR

This is another move in which a player without the ball moves free. It involves a cut by an offensive player towards the basket to the side of the defensive player away from the ball. It is mainly used when the offensive player is being overplayed by the defender or the defender turns to look at the ball. The offensive player reacts to the defence and moves free.

Offence

This move can best be illustrated with some examples.

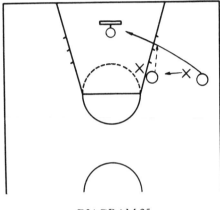

DIAGRAM 25

When the ball is being held by a high post player and the defender marking a forward turns to help mark the post player, the forward can cut for the basket to receive a pass from the post player (diagram 25).

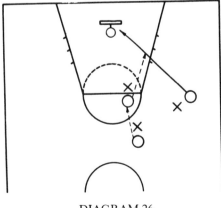

DIAGRAM 26

This manoeuvre can be a three-player move in a situation where the offensive guard has the ball and finds that the passing lane to the forward is overplayed by the defender marking the forward, but that the passing lane into a high post player is open. The pass is made in to the post and the forward cuts for the basket to receive a pass from the post player (diagram 26).

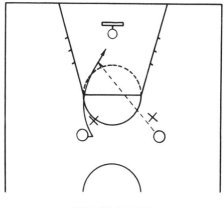

DIAGRAM 27

The backdoor move can be employed by a guard, when his co-guard has the ball and the defender is overplaying the pass to the guard without the ball. This guard without the ball should break to the basket for the lead pass (diagram 27).

Defence

A simple method of countering a team that is employing a backdoor type of move is for the defender to discontinue overplaying the passing lane to his opponent. However, overplaying a passing lane is a legitimate defensive tactic, but care should be taken when executing it that a player near the ball is not left completely free. Against the first situation, in which the ball was held by the post player, the forward can give help to his team-mate by sagging back towards the post with the ball, but he should maintain a view of his opponent and retain a position closer to the basket than the offensive forward. If the forward starts to cut, the defender should ignore the post player and concentrate on marking his man.

Against the three-man play, the defender marking the forward should adjust his defensive position faster when the ball is passed into the post, so that he is between his man and the basket. Against the guard-to-guard move, the defender marking the guard who is cutting backdoor should know when the opponent starts to cut, even though he is overplaying the passing lane. When the guard cuts, the defender should ignore the ball and follow his man with both hands up to take away the passing lanes. When overplaying a passing lane, the defender should be off line, in a stance facing the opponent and with the arm nearest the player with the ball up, with his hand in the direct passing lane. With this stance, using peripheral vision to see the ball and his opponent, the defender is prepared for the backdoor type of cut. Against any backdoor move by the offensive team, sagging and floating defensive team-mates, who are giving defensive support, should be prepared to help out and pick up cutters who are free in the area under the basket.

FIGURE 19

PICK SCREEN

Offence

Screens can be established and used in a number of different situations in a game and it is impossible here to illustrate all the screen situations that could occur during a game.

A commonly-used screen is the pick screen — a screen set at the side of the team-mate's opponent.

Figure 19 illustrates one guard setting a screen for a team-mate to use. The screen is set by player no. 10 to the side of the defender. It may be necessary to set the screen slightly behind the defender and in these situations the screen should be set a metre away from the defender. The guard with the ball drives close to his team-mate for the basket. Diagram 28 shows this manoeuvre.

FIGURE 19

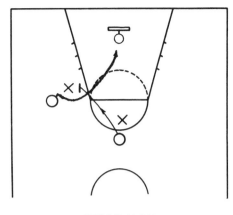

DIAGRAM 28

In any pick screen situation the player using the screen attempts to run his defender into it. The screening player, if moving when used, will be penalized for any contact that may occur, so responsibility is with the screening player to make the screen effective.

Diagram 29 illustrates a forward-to-guard screen.

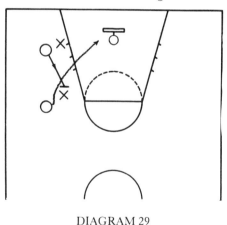

DIAGRAM 29

Defence

Screen situations can be defended in one of three ways: the defender marking the man using the screen will go 'over the top'; the defender will use a 'slide' manoeuvre, i.e. move between the player setting the screen and a fellow defender; or the defenders may 'switch', i.e. the team-mate who is marking the screening player changes his defensive assignment and marks the opponent of the team-mate whose progress has been impeded; this team-mate is now responsible for marking the screener. All these defences against screen situations will depend upon the defenders communicating with each other. The defender marking the offensive player setting the screen is responsible for giving his team-mate a warning that the screen has been set. The defender marking the possible driver should by then be alert to the screen, maybe putting a hand back to feel where the screen is stationed. If the offensive player with the ball is a good outside shot, the defender should make an effort to go 'over the top' and stay between opponent and basket. To avoid fouling and having his progress impeded by the screen, the defender should straighten up as he goes past the screen, bending his knees to take up his basic defensive stance once he has avoided the screen.

Defending the Screen situation

Going over the top

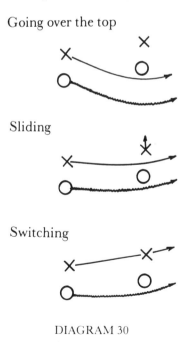

Sliding

Switching

DIAGRAM 30

FIGURE 20

If the man he is marking does not have a good outside shot, he can safely use the 'slide' to avoid the screen. Here the defender being screened, on hearing from his team-mate that the screen has been set, should sag slightly, as should his team-mate marking the screener. The defender marking the player with the ball now has space to move through between screen and the basket, and he can be helped in this movement by his team-mate physically guiding him through. Figure 20 illustrates the slide being used to defend a post play. Defender no. 11 slides between his team-mate and the post, and is thus able to stay with his opponent. Note that the defender, no. 5, who is marking the post, steps back to allow his team-mate room to slide through.

Should the screen be effective and the defender's progress be impeded to a degree where he finds it impossible to follow his man, then the defenders switch. The defender marking the screener takes the player moving free and the defender who has been screened quickly established his defensive position against the player who has set the screen.

In defensive situations involving an offensive player dribbling off a screen, the defender who is marking the screen can give help to his defensive team-mate who is being screened by shifting slightly into the path of the player making use of the screen. This movement towards the path of the driving player will force the driver to move away from the basket, so giving his defence man more time to recover and thus avoid the screen. However, this is not a switch. Should the screener roll, the defender who is marking the screening offensive player, having delayed the driver and given his team-mate time, should turn and concentrate on stopping passes in to the rolling player. When he moves into the path of the driving player, he should keep one hand touching the screener, so

FIGURE 20

that, when he does roll, the movement is immediately felt by the defender. Diagram 31 illustrates this move.

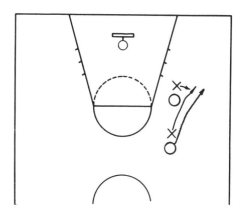

DIAGRAM 31

PICK AND ROLL

Offence

Should the defender marking the player setting the screen switch on to the offensive player moving free, then the screener should roll. In the pick and roll, one offensive player sets the screen and, as he is used and the defenders switch, he pivots (rolls) so as to move to the basket facing his team-mate throughout the move. Figure 21 shows a forward (no. 11), setting a pick screen for his team-mate and, as the defender (no. 5) switches to mark the dribbler, the screen (no. 11) executes the roll and moves to the basket to receive a pass from his team-mate. The offensive team is taking advantage of the poor position that the defender who has been screened is in. The player who has set the screen can, as he is aware that the screen is being effected, pivot to put the defender on his back. This may be before the switch has occurred. He then moves to the basket looking for a pass.

FIGURE 21

Defence

The best defence against a team that is screening and rolling in for passes is not to allow the screen to be effective and so force the defence to have to switch. The switch should not become a manoeuvre used by a lazy defender, who allows himself to be beaten by the screen. Should the screen be effective even with maximum effort by the defender, then the switch may be necessary. The player who has been screened out calls the switch; his team-mate takes the player driving free. The player who has been screened out should follow the player rolling for the basket in the same way as when defending the offensive player who has used a backdoor play — that is he is concentrating attention on the offensive player and following him closely, with arms up. If the offensive team is using, during each offensive, a pattern of play that involves screens in similar positions on court, the defensive team can use a jump switch. In this the defender who is switching to take the driving player jumps quickly into the path of the driver in an effort to gain the charging foul. Provided that the defender can establish his defensive position, be stationary and arrive at the spot first, and that the driver causes contact, then the driver is responsible for the foul.

POST PLAY

The origin of the name of 'post play' has been covered earlier in chapter 3.

Offence

This is an offensive manoeuvre in which a player takes up a position usually with his back to the basket he is attacking, thus providing a target to receive a pass and/or act as a rear screen to enable a team-mate to run his opponent into the post player. In figure 22 the player (no. 11) has moved to receive the pass in a post position near to the key. The guard who has passed the ball cuts close to the post player, running his opponent into the post player in the process, and takes the hand-off pass from the post, then drives in to the basket for the shot. Points to note are that the post player should receive the pass as he arrives at the post position. He takes the ball with his back to the basket, thus giving protection to it, and then the cutter moves close to the post player so that there is no room for the defender to follow him.

In figure 22 it should be noted that the post player, having passed to the cutter, moves in for the rebound or possible return pass.

The post player may, as in figure 22, after establishing the post, pivot to face the basket, then his team-mate still cuts close to him and receives the pass.

If the post player has moved out to receive the pass, the cutter is moving into an area of court that was left clear when the post player moved out. This is illustrated in diagram 32, which shows a post play.

FIGURE 22

The post player can also be used as a rear screen for the guard to use on a dribbling manoeuvre in which he brushes his defender off on the post. In this move the post does not handle the ball.

Defence

The first point in defence in a post play is to prevent the ball being passed in to the post player. Should the pass be made into the post, the defender marking the player who has passed should sag. This, together with a warning received from his team-mate, will enable him to avoid the post and he should be able to go 'over the top'. The defensive manoeuvres used against pick screens can also be used to defend the post plays and figure 22 illustrates the defender marking the player using the screen sliding through.

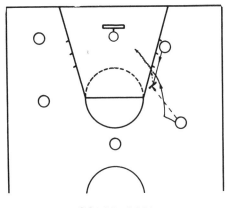

DIAGRAM 32

FIGURE 22

SPLITTING THE POST

Offence

This is usually a three-man play in which two offensive players cut from opposite sides and close to a post player in an effort to elude their opponents. Usually the player who passes the ball into the post player will be the first cutter and the post player looks to pass the ball to the first team-mate who has lost his opponent in the congestion of the scissors action. This pass will usually be to the second cutter, as the first cutter is a sacrifice man. The action can occur with two guards cutting past a player in a high post position at the free throw line, or by a guard and a forward, when the post is situated mid-way down the side of the key. Diagrams 33 and 34 respectively illustrate these moves.

DIAGRAM 33

FIGURE 23

With three players involved there are a number of options that can be worked from the basic play.

Figure 23 illustrates a splitting the post move in which the ball is passed from the forward to the post, after the former has received a pass from the guard The guard cuts first and then the forward cuts off the post to take the ball, losing his opponent on the post. Diagram 34 illustrates this move.

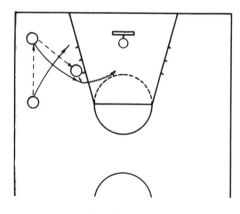

DIAGRAM 34

FIGURE 23

Defence

Defence against splitting the post is the same as for other post plays. Against the post set high, other defenders marking the offensive players not involved in the split should be prepared to help out in the area under the basket. Against the post established at the side of the court, the defence should aim to prevent the ball reaching the post player.

SCREEN OFF THE BALL

Offence

This is another three-man play. The screen is set on the defender of an offensive player who does not have the ball; the latter.then cuts off the screen to receive a pass from a team-mate. Diagram 35 illustrates this screen off the ball move. This play can occur when the offensive team has three players: one a guard and the other players in the high forward area. The guard passes the ball to one forward and then moves over and sets the pick screen for the other forward to use. This forward cuts down the centre of the court for the pass .

FIGURE 24

In figure 24 the ball is passed from guard (no. 7) to his co-guard (no. 11), who passes on to the forward (no. 4). The guard (no. 7) cuts close to the team-mate (no. 5) in a high post position, losing his defender and cutting down the centre of the key to receive a pass from the forward and move in for the shot.

Defence

As this screen is being set against the defender of an opponent who does not have the ball, the defender should not be marking so close that he is unable to follow the player who is using the screen. As with screen and post plays, the warning given by team-mates should enable the screen off the ball to be adequately covered by the defensive team.

Teaching

The basic two- and three-man plays discussed earlier will occur in the game when played by very inexperienced players.

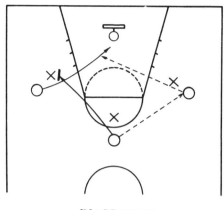

DIAGRAM 35

The manoeuvres will not be by design and the players involved are unlikely to be able to describe in detail how and why the manoeuvre succeeded in freeing a player.

The teacher/coach, when introducing the basic team plays, should initially take advantage of this 'natural' use of the basic team play by allowing his players to play two-versus-two or three-versus-three basketball. When they execute, or nearly execute, one of the basic plays, he should stop their play and demonstrate, by an 'action replay', what happened and how they were able to get a player free.

To teach the players to use the basic two- or three-man plays described earlier, the coach should work his players on one move at a time, have them execute the move initially without defenders, and then introduce some defenders, either active or passive.

In chapter 3 advice was given on teaching cutting and screen plays. The obvious development is for the players to play two-versus-two half court games, attempting to use the particular move they are working on.

6

TEAM DEFENCE

Team defensive play is very dependent upon individual defensive ability. A defensive team's organisation should endeavour to match *offensive* ability with *defensive* ability. Slow players should be marking slow players, tall players against tall players. The deployment should endeavour to have the taller players close to the backboard, so they are in a position to gain defensive rebounds.

The manner in which a team applies the defensive principles mentioned in chapter 4 and any emphasis given to certain principles are reflected in differing team tactics. The main different team defensive tactics are man-to-man defensive organisation and zone defensive organisation. Although these two systems have different features, a good team defence will endeavour to make use of the advantages of both in their 'straight' form, although it should be noted that there is no such thing as a straight man-to-man defence or a straight zone defence — each makes use of the other's defensive concept. The basic concept of a man-to-man defence is that the defenders mark an assigned opponent and not the ball; the basic concept of a zone defence is that the defence works as a team marking the ball. For success it should be remembered that both depend on each *individual* defender's ability to play *individual defence*.

MAN-TO-MAN DEFENCE

Each defender is responsible for one opponent, usually marking between the offensive player and the basket. Depth is given to the defence by the defenders marking offensive players away from the ball. These players adjust their position so that they are still between their man and the basket, but they move towards the ball so that they can help out, if necessary, and give any support. This involves the use of sagging to the basket to be ready to cover team-mates.

The defenders marking primary pass receivers will sag slightly from their opponents, but they must be prepared to move up to the opponent just as they receive the pass. Players marking opponents away from the ball should sag towards the basket and move slightly laterally towards the ball, so that they can see both their opponent and the ball and are stationed in a good position to cover an opponent, who may free himself from a defender and move towards the basket to receive the ball for a shot. The defender's attitude should not be 'he is not my man', but rather 'any offensive player moving in for a shot unmarked is my man'. To help players work together as a team, they should be encouraged to talk to each other. This talking on defence is particularly important in combating screen situations. The defender being screened should attempt to avoid the screen, because of the warning received from a team-mate. He avoids the screen by going 'over the top' or by sliding through. Very occasionally defenders will switch, but this should not occur out of laziness; defenders in screen situations should make every effort to stay with their man.

The man-to-man defence that has been described so far could be called a sagging man-to-man defence. The defenders can move out from the basket and put more pressure on their opponents by close marking. However, the weakness of the straight man-to-man close-marking defence is that there is no depth, and one weak defender will be difficult to cover. A close-marking defence that is based upon man-to-man is a pressing man-to-man — this can be played over the whole court. In a pressing man-to-man defence the ball will be marked by a defender, who may endeavour to force the player with the ball to dribble towards the side lines; whenever the dribble stops, a nearby defensive team-mate will leave his man and come quickly to double-team the player with the ball. The defenders marking offensive players without the ball take up a position to prevent passes being made to the men they are marking. Diagram 36 illustrates a man-to-man pressure defence, the positioning of defenders and a double team occurring.

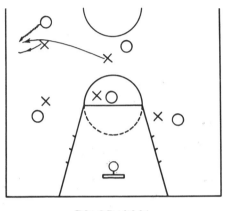

DIAGRAM 36

The man-to-man pressure defence requires talented, fast defensive players.

Teaching Man-to-Man Defence

The initial game played by beginners will be using a man-to-man defence, but, as the offensive players improve, the defence can be taught to play a half court man-to-man defence. This involves them quickly retreating to their defensive half at the loss of possession and only marking their opponent when he comes over the half-way line. Working from this, the sagging man-to-man can be taught.

ZONE DEFENCE

Each defender in a zone defence is concerned with the ball and is responsible for guarding a particular area (zone) on the court — this is usually near to the basket, in the high percentage scoring area. The team will work from a basic defensive formation, for example, 2:1:2, 1:3:1, 3:2, or 2:3. As with the terminology for offensive formations, the defensive numbering is from the centre of the court towards the basket, thus the three-two zone has three players at the front of the defence, stationed across the area of the free throw line, and two players in the area under the basket. The defensive formation used is a point of reference, and enables the players in the defence to establish responsibility for particular areas of court and offensive players in their area. The players they are responsible for change with the movement of the offensive players, but the defence is endeavouring to ensure that the ball-handler is marked on a straight man-to-man basis, that potential pass receivers are marked and that there is defensive depth to the man marking the ball-handler.

The offensive team is endeavouring to take a shot from as close to the basket as possible. The closer they move to the basket for their shot, the higher the percentage of their shots they are likely to score. In zone defence the defenders usually station themselves close to the basket, covering the high percentage scoring area and establishing, as a team unit, a good formation to prevent passes being made to opponents who have moved into the danger area. In this way the defenders force their opponents to take shots from outside the 15 feet range — a range at which most inexperienced players will be unsuccessful.

As with man-to-man offence, there are certain floor formations used by zone defences. The more skilled teams using zone defence may aim to vary their basic zone defence formation to match the pattern of the offence, so that they have the advantages of both man-to-man and zone defence.

A commonly-played zone defence is the 2:1:2 zone and a study of how this zone can be used by club teams will illustrate some aspects of zone defence. This formation has two defenders at the front, taking up positions based on points at the end of the free throw line; two defenders are stationed in front of the backboard, one at each side, with the fifth defender stationed in the middle of the key, half-way between the other two pairs. With the ball being held by an opponent in the guard position (player 3), all the defenders should move towards the ball. If the offensive guard is in the middle of the court, he will find himself marked by the two front players in the zone — these two front men in the zone are often referred to as the 'hustlers' of the zone. Footwork is important for these two defenders, as they also have to cover their respective sides of the court, near the free throw line. Their stance should be such that the foot they have forward is the inside foot — that is the foot nearer to the middle of the court. From this stance they should be able to move quickly to the side. If the ball should be passed to a player at the side of the court (2 in the diagram), one of the front two defenders must move to the ball. The rest of the zone defenders should also move towards the ball. With the ball in this position, it can be seen in diagram 37 that the zone defenders can, with little adjustment, also mark the potential pass receivers (3 and 1 in the diagram). One of the two front players in the zone defence has moved to the ball in this illustration, while the other moves to the middle of the free throw line. The defender in the zone under the basket to the side of the ball will have adjusted his position slightly, so that he is marking the potential pass receiver in his zone of responsibility, i.e. the player (1) in the corner. The offensive players (4) and (5), stationed on the opposite side of the court, can be left practically unmarked. The defender in the area under the basket furthest away from the ball will move towards the ball, but he will also adjust his position to see all offensive players, so that movement of offensive players from the weak side can be covered. Should an offensive player start to move from the weak side into the middle of the key, this defender away from the ball should give verbal warnings to his team-mates and, if necessary, mark the offensive player. The defender in the middle of the zone will be in a position to cover his four team-mates in case they are beaten on a drive by an offensive player. To discourage penetrating passes the zone defenders should keep their arms up and moving.

Against this zone the offensive team will frequently station a player in the zone, playing either high or low post. If he is playing low, he will usually be moving from side to side of the restricted area. This is when talking by defenders is critical. If one of the back men in the zone has to mark a forward in a corner with the ball, and he has an offensive post player in his zone, then the middle man in the zone is responsible for the offensive post as in diagram 38.

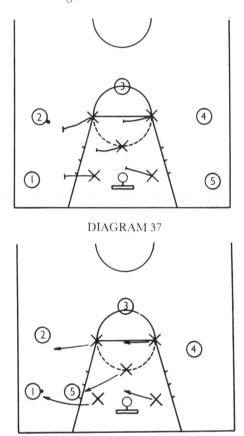

DIAGRAM 37

DIAGRAM 38

If the ball now moves round the zone, but the offensive post player does not move, the middle man in the zone moves across, following the ball, and the back man, who was marking the forward, now moves in to mark the post player. This is shown in diagram 39.

Zone defence is very much a team effort. Players, particularly the hustlers at the front of the zone, must be prepared to work hard and it bears repeating that *talking between players is essential.*

The zone aims to cover the area of the key and to stop the ball being passed in to a post player. If the post player does receive the ball, they attempt to double-team the post, so that he cannot shoot or make an easy pass out. As the zone defence is marking the ball, they should be alert to opportunities to intercept it.

Another popular zone defence is the 1:3:1 zone defence. Diagram 40 illustrates the basic set up of this zone and the areas of responsibility.

The 2:3 zone is particularly strong in the area under the basket and in the corner. The basic set-up and areas of responsibility of this zone are shown in diagram 41.

The 3:2 zone, although very strong at the front, has weaknesses once the front line has been penetrated. The areas of responsibility of this zone are shown in diagram 42.

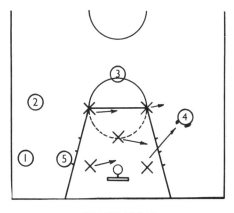

DIAGRAM 39

In playing a zone defence the following points can act as a useful check-list for the coach. A zone defence should have:

(a) The *ball* marked man to man.
(b) The next potential pass receivers marked man-to-man.
(c) The man marking the ball-handler should be covered, so that the defence has depth.
(d) The centre of the free-throw line should always be marked.

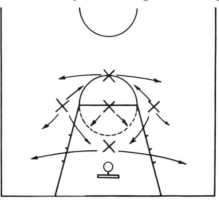

DIAGRAM 40

(*e*)   The defender in the zone furthest away from the ball should be able to see all the offensive players.

(*f*)   On each pass all five defenders should move, making sure that they are moving to a pass and not a fake.

(*g*)   An offensive player who moves into the area under the basket must be marked man-to-man.

Zone Press

Working with a zone defence, it is possible to play pressure tactics against the opponents. Pressure tactics aim to force an

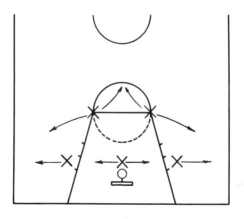

DIAGRAM 41

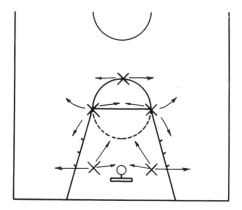

DIAGRAM 42

error by the opposing team, particularly the passing error or 10 seconds rule violation, or to gain a 5 seconds, held ball situation. A zone press can operate from different formations. In a 3:1:1 full court zone press, which can be set up after a score, the middle man endeavours to encourage the in-bounds ball to the side. The opponent who receives the ball in bounds is marked man-to-man and, if he does dribble, he is steered towards the side line. The middle man at the front of the zone moves in to double-team on the player with the ball. The other man in the front three covers the nearest potential receiver and the other two defenders take up positions to cover the long pass down the court. Diagram 43 illustrates the 3:1:1 zone defence in use.

In the zone press the defence is endeavouring to create a situation where they can double-team the ball-handler — this will occur in certain areas of the court; the most suitable being the corners of each half court. In these areas the court boundary lines create an additional line of defence and enable the double team to be more effective.

Pressing defences are gambling defences and require team work and fast active defenders, so they should not be introduced to inexperienced players.

Teaching 2:1:2 Zone Defence

In teaching this zone the coach could draw chalk circles on the floor, with the centres of the circles situated at the points

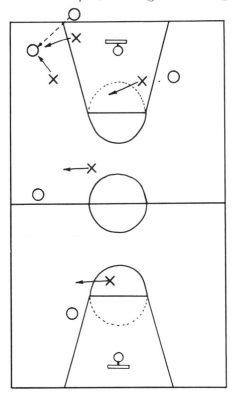

DIAGRAM 43

indicated, for stationing the defenders. The circles should have a radius of about 6 feet (see diagram 44). To teach the movements of the defenders, station five attacking players in a horse-shoe formation, with the ball at the guard in the centre of the court. With the ball in this position, all defenders should move towards the ball as far as the edge of their circles. The ball is now marked by the two defenders at the front of the defence. If the ball is then passed to a player at the side of the horse-shoe, the defenders have to adjust again by moving to the edge of their 'circles' nearest the ball, thus the ball is still marked by one of the front players in the zone. With the ball in this position, the point can be made that the zone defenders should endeavour to mark the next potential pass receiver. One front man is marking the ball, while the other remains in the centre of the court, marking the player who has just passed the ball. The ball will be moved round the offensive horse-shoe formation, checking before each pass is made that the defence has moved correctly. Another pass is made and the defence checked again. After going through this routine and ensuring that the players know their movements, the offensive team can be told to try to score. The defence is now working against fully active offensive players.

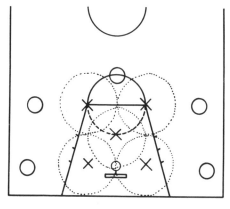

DIAGRAM 44

7

TEAM OFFENCE

In this and previous chapters team offence and defence are considered. This treatment under two headings, 'offence' and 'defence', is not intended to give the impression to the reader that each is totally distinct from the other. Offence depends upon defence and defence will depend upon offence. How the team offence is organised will obviously depend upon the team defence employed by the opponents.

Details of the principles of play on offence, the one-versus-one situation and some of the basic two-and-three man team plays, have been covered in earlier chapters. In this chapter some forms of offence will be studied as examples of ways in which the basics mentioned earlier in the book are put together.

FLOOR FORMATION

Basketball is a game in which all members of the team are involved in both offence and defence. Inexperienced teams interpret offence as all five players chasing the ball. The importance of spreading out and of players accepting their role of playing on offence without the ball has already been mentioned. The three basic court playing positions were introduced in chapter 1, but, before moving on to consider specific offences, these floor positions will be reviewed.

Guards

Guards play facing the basket, in the area of the court from the free-throw line back towards the half-way line. They will usually be the shorter players on the team and will need to develop a good drive, be first-class ball-handlers and be good shots from the 15-25 foot range. More experienced players are useful here, as in this position on the floor they can see the remainder of the players and can, therefore, act as 'floor generals' directing play. In the guard position, a player is his team's safety player — not only the first line of defence. He should also be in a position to receive a pass when an offensive play breaks down but possession is not lost, so that a new offensive move can be started.

Forwards

Forwards play facing the basket, in the area of the court from the free-throw line to the end line, but usually outside the restricted area. Forwards will be some of the taller players on the team, good rebounders and have a good drive and shot from the side and corner of the court.

Post Players

These are usually the tallest members of the team and they work close to the basket to take advantage of their height. They play in and around the key, although, of course, the 3 seconds rule limits the time a player may actually spend in the restricted area. The post players should be good rebounders, able to shoot when closely marked and safe ball-handlers when closely marked. They need to develop good footwork to be able to free themselves in the area under the basket to receive a pass and to create a post or screen for a team-mate to use.

The distribution and placing of players on the team's offence will vary according to the players on the team and the way the defensive team is playing. A basketball 'shorthand' is used to describe the formation of the team and indicate the number of players who are playing in each area of the court. Three commonly used floor formations are: 2:1:2, 3:2 and

1:3:1. The first number refers to the area furthest from the basket being attacked, i.e. the guard area. The 2:1:2 formation has two guards, one post player and two forwards. This type of offence may be used by a team with two small players and three tall players, or one tall player and four small players. Diagram 45 shows this formation.

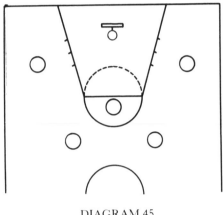

DIAGRAM 45

The 1:3:1 formation will be used by a team with three short players and two tall players. The two tall players play the post position, with one high at the free-throw line and the other low, near to the basket. The other three players play outside the key (diagram 46).

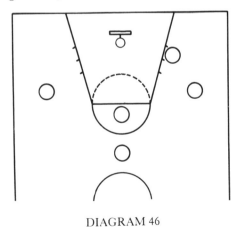

DIAGRAM 46

The 3:2 formation will be used by a team with three small players and two taller players. The three small players take up guard positions and the two taller players play as forwards, who will on occasions move into the post area (diagram 47).

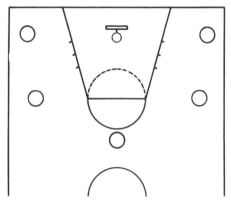

DIAGRAM 47

These are not rigid formations — positions are fluid and during the course of the game players will often exchange places. The guard may, for example, drive for the basket but not beat his man and end up in a forward position, while the forward from this area moves out to replace the driver in the guard position.

In this book two examples of team offence from two different formations will be shown and possible moves that can operate from these formations will be mentioned. Throughout these examples the two- and three-player moves mentioned earlier are used and the reader should refer back to the pages where these moves were covered. The offensive moves discussed are those used against a man-to-man defence. Diagrams will be used to illustrate each move and the number against the players mentioned in the text refers to their number in the diagram.

THREE-TWO OFFENCE

This is a horse-shoe formation, with three small players as

guards and two taller players as forwards who are capable of playing in the post area.

Beginning with a 'give and go' (see page 128) the ball is passed to a guard (no. 2) at the side and then on to the forward (no. 1), who has stepped out to the corner. The guard (no. 2) who made this pass cuts to the basket to look for the return pass (diagram 48). Should this cutting guard (no. 2) not receive a pass, he continues through and under the basket to set a screen on the defender marking the forward (no. 5) on the opposite side of the court. While this is happening, the guard position vacated by the cutter is filled by the guard (no. 3) who started the action. When he has moved, he receives a pass out from the forward (no. 1) in the corner. The forward (no. 5) on the weak side makes use of the screen and moves across, in front of the basket, looking for a pass (diagram 49).

Should the pass not come, this forward (no. 5) continues across the key and establishes a post position mid-way down the key. The pass is then made in to this forward (no. 5), who has established a post position, and the guard (no. 3) who makes the pass in and the other forward (no. 1) execute a split action (see page 141) on the post (diagram 50). Should this not

DIAGRAM 48

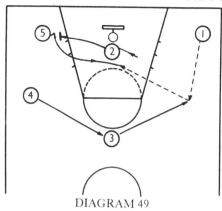

DIAGRAM 49

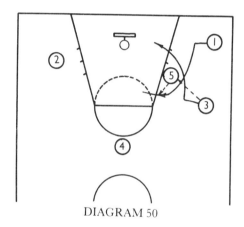

DIAGRAM 50

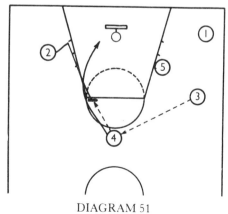

DIAGRAM 51

lead to a score or if it is not possible to pass in to the forward (no. 5) who has established the post, the ball should be passed out to the guard (no. 4), who will have moved out to a position in the middle of the court. This guard (no. 4) then passes to the guard (no. 2) who was the first cutter. Guard no. 2 having set a high post on the weak side of the court, the player who passes in to this post cuts for the basket close to the post, looking for a return pass (diagram 51).

TWO-ONE-TWO FORMATION

Two guards, one post player and two forwards are used. Most of the offensive moves included in the chapter on two- and three-player moves can be used from this offensive formation. The guard (no. 2) can pass to the forward (no. 1) and cut for the basket on a give and go type of move (diagram 52). Should the guard (no. 2) not get free, he can move to the corner of the court and, with the post player (no. 5) moving down the same side of the court, a triangle will be formed, and they can execute a split on the post, as in the three-two offence (diagram 50). The two guards (nos 2 and 3) can also execute a splitting the post move by passing in to the post (no. 5) and executing the split. However, from this position the defenders marking the forwards can help to cover any offensive player who has moved free on the post scissors action (diagram 33). It is more usual to use one guard (no. 3) to cut off the post player (no. 5) (diagram 53). Screen plays can be executed by guards screening for each other: no. 2 screens for no. 3. Then the post player moves down the side of the key to clear a space for this drive, which may not go all the way for a lay-up shot, but may finish with a jump shot from the free-throw line. A forward (no. 4) can move up to set a screen for a guard (no. 3) to use (diagram 29) for a pick and roll play.

Offensive players do not remain in the same position — exchanges of position occur frequently. Coaches should develop their own team offence using the two- and three-man plays mentioned in chapter 5. Teaching the team offence can occur initially with no defenders in position, then with passive defenders and finally in a game situation, perhaps using a half-court game.

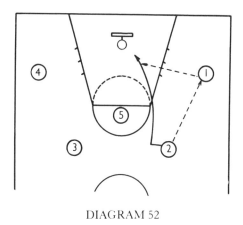

DIAGRAM 52

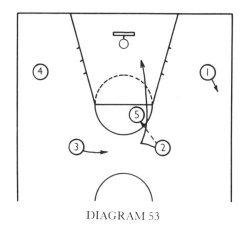

DIAGRAM 53

ATTACKING ZONE DEFENCES

It has been seen that a zone defence aims to assemble the defensive players in a set formation, usually in the area under the basket, each player being responsible for marking a certain zone or area on court. The team works as a unit and moves as a unit with the ball. Thus its main defensive effort is concentrated on giving coverage to the defender who is concerned with marking the player with the ball, so that, if he is beaten, assistance can be given. Additionally, each player is responsible for a zone on the court and marks an opponent who moves into his zone.

A zone defence has a number of weaknesses, which will be considered before any reference to attack is made. These weaknesses are:

1. Because players assemble in a set formation, the fast break is an obvious first weapon against the zone. Only when the fast break has not succeeded will the offensive team organise to attack other weaknesses in the zone defence.
2. The zone defence is weak where the zones of two defenders meet, therefore the offensive team should go down court and set up a different formation to the one adopted by the zone.
3. The ball can move faster than players, therefore it is possible to out-manoeuvre the defence with rapid passing.
4. A defender responsible for a certain zone will have a problem if two attacking players stand within or near his zone.
5. Finally and most important, most zone defences cover the area under the basket; they can, therefore, be beaten by a team with players capable of shooting and scoring over the zone.

The defending team, by playing zone defence, has presented the offensive team with a problem. If the offensive team has no players who can shoot and score consistently from the 15 foot plus range, then the zone has succeeded, because it has prevented the offensive team from shooting from the danger area close to the basket. The offensive team will then have to score its points from the fast break, which is unlikely to be sufficient to win the game. The zone defence, through the concentration of players in the area under the basket; makes passes and drives into this area difficult. The offensive team, if it is to score against a zone defence, must have players who can score from a range of 15-18 foot from the basket. The offensive ideas given below assume that the offence has players with this shooting ability. When attacking against a zone defence, the offensive team will use some of the following methods of attack:

(*a*) When the team possesses shooting ability, the simplest attack is for the offensive players to spread round the outside of the defence and pass the ball around until one of them has a shooting opportunity. This will involve little or no movement of the players, as the ball does the work. The offensive players are unlikely to have much time to take their shots and they should, therefore, take a stance, so that they can shoot immediately they receive the ball. This means that the offensive players should threaten the goal by facing the basket and passes should be directed in front of the offensive player who is free to shoot.

(*b*) The use of shooting ability can be helped further if the offensive team is stationed so that, when they face the basket, they are attacking a point between two defenders, i.e. where their 'zones' meet. This will present a problem to the defenders who mark the offensive player. If neither defender marks the offensive player when he has the ball, a shooting chance occurs. If both defenders move out to mark, then there should be another offensive player free. If one defender moves out to mark, he will be at the edge of his zone and an opportunity will be presented for another offensive player to step into the gap. In diagram 54, if no. 2 has the ball and no. 1 moves out to mark, no. 1 can step into the gap and is free to receive a pass.

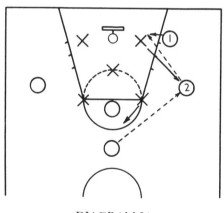

DIAGRAM 54

(*c*) When the defender moves out of his zone, an offensive player should step into the gap presented. Zone defence being a team effort, a serious weakness will exist in the zone if one player makes a mistake and leaves his zone unmarked. If the offensive team moves a player into the gap and then a pass is made to this player, a scoring opportunity or confusion in the 'team defence' will occur, because another defender will have to give a team-mate an unhindered shot. For example, a team should be alert to members of the zone moving away quickly for premature, steal-away, one-man, fast breaks. If this occurs, the defence is weak and, if the offensive team can obtain the rebound, then a spot is available for a shot.

(*d*) A front screen can be set on a defender in a zone defence to give a team-mate an unhindered shot. For example, a forward (no. 1) in the corner can be helped by a post player (no. 5), who sets a screen at the edge of the restricted area, between the forward and the basket. (This is illustrated in Diagram 55). The defender marking this zone will be screened and the forward (no. 1) will then have a shooting opportunity. If the defender steps around the screen and marks the forward (no. 1) with the ball, the screener is now possibly free for a pass. In this situation it is preferable that the screener should not move once he has set the screen, other than to pivot to face the basket if he receives the ball. If he moves out towards the forward, there will be insufficient space for the two offensive players to work. If he moves towards the basket after the defender has gone round him, the screener is likely to break the 3 seconds rule or make it easier for another defensive player to help mark him.

(*e*) With the zone moving as a team unit to cover movements of the ball, it is possible to out-manoeuvre it by rapid passing, as the ball can be passed faster than the defenders can move. Movement of the ball is important in any basketball offensive situation. Against man-to-man defence, it is usual for the offensive team to pass and then move. Against a zone defence, however, a useful offence is to do the opposite of the defenders — as they move, the offence stands still. Of course, it is not intended that players should never move any more than, when playing against a man-to-man defence, players never stand still. Mention has already been made of a player moving into a gap created by the defender leaving his zone. Occasionally (as in diagram 56), after passing to a team-mate, an offensive player will cut into the zone, towards the basket, looking for a return pass. This may cause the defender

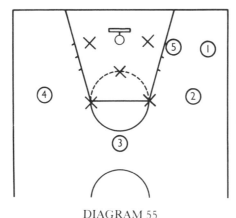

DIAGRAM 55

(2) to move back and leave a space for an offensive player (no. 3) to step in to receive the ball and be free for a shot. The cutter, on odd occasions, may be left free, and the return pass made in a give and go movement.

(*f*) The give and go for the return pass is unlikely to be very effective against a zone defence, as the defence aims to cover the area under the basket, preventing passes or drives into it. Should a zone defence leave the area of the key near the basket free, the offensive team should exploit this weakness by moving a player into the gap for a pass. Timing of this move is critical and the player moving into the gap should receive the pass as he arrives in the free space. This move should employ the next method of attacking a zone defence — the weakness of the blind side of the zone.

(*g*) A zone defence, moving as a unit with the ball, must look at the ball first and the man second. This is opposite to the man-to-man defence, where the primary object of attention is the man. With the zone defence, this means that the offensive team should station a player behind the defence, usually along the base line. A player in this position will cause a problem to defenders. Do they follow and move to the ball or do they stay with the man? The offensive players will find opportunities to exploit this use of the blind side of the defence, if combined with limited movement by players on offence. Defensive players moving in response to the

movement of the ball will occasionally forget about this
offensive player, who can then step into the gap because the
defenders, who are not anticipating the move, have their
attention focussed on the ball. He can then be passed the ball

DIAGRAM 56

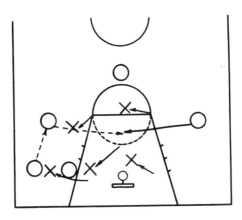

DIAGRAM 57

and given an opportunity of shooting. The ball and the player should arrive at the spot at the same time. He should not, therefore, move until he sees that his team-mate is ready to pass.

(*h*) Mention has been made of the weakness of the zone defence, when two offensive players are within the zone of responsibility of one defender. This 'overload' is achieved in offence by creating two-on-one or, more likely, three-on-two situations and using a floor formation of offensive players that gives this relationship relative to the defensive formation. For example, an overload can be achieved down one side of the court, if a zone defence is organised with two defenders at the front of the zone (one marking a zone centred at the end of the free throw line), with two other defenders near the basket (one at each side) and the fifth defender in the middle of the restricted area. If the offensive team sets up players for the use of the screen mentioned earlier ([d] and illustrated in diagram 55) and stations a third offensive player at the side of the court opposite the free-throw line, a three-versus-two situation will be created against the zone defence on that side. If the centre man in the zone moves over to help out, the middle of the restricted area is free for a player (no. 4) from the 'blind side' of the zone to step in (diagram 57). If the ball is being played down the side of the court where the overload occurs, the blind side will be on the opposite side of the court. The player from this blind side moves into the gap and stops, receives the pass and, if free, he shoots.

(*j*) Finally, although few one-versus-one opportunities will be created for a player with the ball, the offensive player with the ball can create problems for the defenders, if use is made of the one- or two-bounce dribble into the zone past a defender. The defenders will collapse onto this player and prevent the shot, but, in collapsing, they will frequently leave another offensive player free for a pass and successful shot. This is an example of penetration of the defence by the offensive team. Against zone defence, the offensive team should endeavour to get the ball inside to a post player or to a player who has cut to that area before taking the outside shot. If the ball goes in to a post player who finds himself marked, he should look for chances to pass the ball out to the other side of the floor. The dribble should be used sparingly against a zone defence.

8

FAST BREAK

In the fast break the offensive team aims to develop the offence quickly to obtain a numerical advantage before the opponents get their defence organised. This type of offence is attractive to watch and even more enjoyable to play. The offence starts immediately the team gains possession of the ball, which could be in its back court, from a stolen pass or a defensive rebound. The simplest fast break is for a player to break down court and have the ball thrown to him while he has the numerical advantage of one-versus-none. However, the danger with this type of fast break is that the breaking offensive player deserts his defensive assignment, leaving his team-mates one short. The opponents are unlikely to allow this type of fast break to continue, as they will instruct a player to watch this break and go with the breaking player as he moves. The offensive team will need to build up their fast break with more players, and this can consist of two players simply breaking down court to receive a long pass. Again this can be a weakness, as the opponents can see the ball coming. Rather than breaking down court, the players not involved in the defensive rebound should move to the side of court, making it easier for the rebounder to make the outlet pass. If the fast-breaking team has a player stationed on each side of the court, then the player who does not receive the ball should cut to mid-court, where he will receive a pass or be in a position to accompany his team-mate, should he dribble down court. Figure 25 illustrates this move and the position for the reception of the outlet pass, which should be opposite the free-throw line. The outlet pass made to a player in this area should be in front of the player, so that he may immediately move the ball down court, either by a pass to a team-mate or with a dribble. Figure 25 illustrates the player (no. 11) moving out to the side of the court to receive the outlet pass and his turn down to look for a breaking team-mate.

Five players on court, working as a team, can gain a numerical advantage by changing quickly from defence to offence at the change of possession. Once the ball has been obtained, either at a rebound or by a steal, the offence starts. First the ball must be moved away from the opponents or the congested area under the backet. To do the latter, the ball can be passed or dribbled to the side of the court. However, this is not critical, as the prime objective is to get the ball down the court. The player who has obtained the ball may find that he can, on landing, start the move down the court on the dribble. The important thing is that opponents who are changing from offence to defence must be avoided — frequently they will be moving down the middle of the court.

The ball is taken down the court using passes or on the dribble. The latter can sometimes be the best, as too many mistakes can occur in an exchange of passes. The success of a fast break depends upon the attitude of mind of the players. The player 'leading' the attack with the ball must not be left alone. Offensive team-mates should strive to get in on the break. As they move down the court, they should spread out and preferably two players should occupy the lanes alongside the man with the ball (figure 26). These lanes are 10-15 feet apart — one lane goes down the middle and one down each side of the court. Players fill the three lanes on a fast break, with the ball being dribbled down the middle. A danger is that the team moving the ball down the court will go too fast and lose control. The break should be quick, but controlled.

As the offence moves to the offensive end, the team must appreciate that it is aiming for the first 'good' shot. If this is a lay-up shot, well and good, but, if the opportunity is presented for an uninterrupted 10-15 foot shot, it should be taken.

FIGURE 25

FIGURE 26

Defenders must be presented with a 'problem' in preventing this good shot, which means the offence attacks the basket and the defence is committed as in figure 27.

To beat the defence, the offensive team should aim to spread out, take the first good shot and make as few passes as possible, and the player with the ball should drive all the way for the basket and only pass off when stopped. Should passes be necessary, they must be crisp and made to a team-mate so that he can easily handle the ball and, if appropriate, move in quickly to take the shot. Above all, the offensive team should try to keep the area under the basket free. These principles are of course applicable to all team offence.

To sum up, special features of the fast break are:

1. Gain control of the ball — the most effective fast breaks develop from interceptions.

FIGURE 27

2. Attack immediately by moving the ball from the area under the basket as quickly as possible.
3. Get the ball into the opponents' half of the court as quickly as possible, even after they have scored.
4. Bring the ball down court under control.
5. Take the first good shot.
6. Aim to have three players in at the end of the break.
7. Appreciate possession, so that, when the fast break does not lead to a good shot, the player does not force the play under the basket.
8. With three players involved in the initial wave of the fast break, a fourth player (the trailer) should be prepared to cut through, using team-mates as screens, for the pass and shot. The fifth player comes down as a safety player to give some protection should a pass interception occur.

At the end of the break, if the middle man has the ball and passes off to a cutting team-mate, he should then move slightly to the side of the key, away from the man to whom he has passed the ball, in an effort to pull the defence away from the cutting player. The no man's land at the end of the break is near to the top of the key, slightly to the sides, and, as the defenders will usually allow room in this area, it should be attacked.

DEFENCE AGAINST THE FAST BREAK

As the offensive team is aiming to gain a numerical advantage and to get behind the defence, an essential point to make on defending the fast break is not to allow this to happen. The simple counter to opponents who are breaking fast against you is to make a fast break defensively. This demands that players respond instantly to the change of possession. While on offence, the team should aim to make every possession lead to a shot at the basket and, if this shot can be made to score, the fast break becomes more difficult to start. While on offence, the team should keep all opponents occupied, so that one defender will not be able to steal away early down the court for the long pass at the change of possession. Once the shot has been taken, the team should aim to gain possession at the rebound or tip the ball into the basket. Should the opponents gain the rebound, they may now have an opportunity to start a fast break. The player who has rebounded the ball should be marked, so that, rather than endeavouring to start the fast break, he is concerned to protect the ball. The rebounder's potential outlet pass receivers should also be marked, so that the rebounder only has the long pass, which the defensive team should be alert to intercept, or the dribble which will waste time and enable the defence to retreat. Should the opponents make the outlet pass, then the defensive team will be in danger of a successful fast break being developed against them, as the outlet pass will almost certainly take the ball behind some of the defenders. If the ball is near a defender, he can make some effort to delay the break, but the danger is that a commitment of a defender to a man with the ball in the centre of the court could be just what the fast breaking team is aiming to achieve. The defensive fast break, once the ball has reached the outlet pass receiver, should be the aim of the defensive team. As defenders break back they should initially move back to their underbasket area, and only when this area is defended move out to take an opponent. The defenders are now in a position to defend a possible lay-up shot although, maybe, allowing the jump shot. As additional defenders arrive a similar principle is applied, defending from the basket out, with possible lay-up and jump shots defended, but now allowing the long set shot. In an outnumbered situation under their own basket, the defence will endeavour to force the fast breaking team to make an extra pass or to stop the offensive movement — both will consume time and allow the defenders who have been overtaken to recover.

In a two-versus-three, outnumbered situation, the defenders should establish a tandem position: one player just in front of the basket they are defending and the other at the free-throw line. The front defender in the tandem takes the ball, particularly when coming down the middle. Should the middle man pass off to a cutter moving down the side, then the defender under the basket should move out to take the ball and the other defender drop back to cover the area under the basket. If both defenders keep their hands up, they can make the cross-court pass under the basket very difficult for the opposition. Diagram 58 illustrates the tandem defence against three players.

DIAGRAM 58

Teaching and Training

The teaching and training of players to improve their fast break should develop out of the training undertaken to improve passing on the move. An early practice for this is with players, working in pairs or in threes, running from one end of the court to the other and passing the ball between them as they move down the court. There are many different practices to help develop different aspects of the fast break and some suggestions are given below.

Two-Player Break

Two players are stationed at the side of the court with another player under the basket with the ball. The latter player tosses the ball onto the backboard, rebounds and passes out to one of the other two players. The player who does not receive the ball breaks down the court to receive a long pass from his team-mate (diagram 59).

This practice can be developed by having the two players who are to break in the key, and only moving out to the side of the court as the rebound is gained. The outlet pass is now made to one of the players at the side of the court. An alternative to the long pass would be for the second pass to be a short pass and have the two players breaking down the court with interchange of passes.

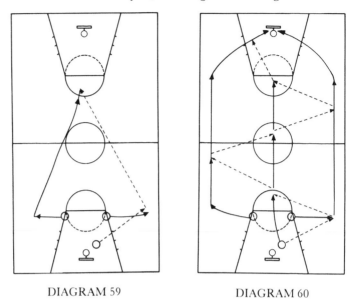

DIAGRAM 59   DIAGRAM 60

Three-Player Break — Passing Straight

This involves the same basic starting set-up as for the two-player break. After the rebounder has passed out, he breaks down the middle and the three players move down the court, passing the ball (diagram 60).

Three-Player Break — Dribble Straight

This has the same start as the previous practice except that, when the player who rebounds receives the ball back in the middle, he dribbles down the centre of the court, stops (using a jump shot) at the D and then passes off to a cutter from the side, who moves in and scores (diagram 61).

Three-Player Break — Passing with Weave

The start is the same as for the previous practice. The player who does not receive the outlet pass breaks to the middle lane and receives a pass from the player who received the outlet pass. The player who rebounded the ball sprints to fill the third lane at the side, as the players move down the court with the ball (diagram 62).

Three-Player Break — Dribble-Weave

This has the same start as the previous practice, but in this instance the player who receives the outlet pass dribbles to mid-court and takes the ball down the centre lane on the dribble. The rebounder follows his outlet pass and cuts down the outside lane (diagram 63).

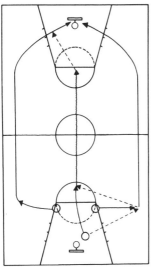

DIAGRAM 61   DIAGRAM 62

Three-Player Break with One Defender

The previous practices involving three players breaking can be carried out with one defender endeavouring to prevent the score. After one wave of three players has gone down court, the player who has gone down the middle becomes the defender for the next three, while the other three players walk back along the side of the court to join the group of players waiting their turn (diagram 64).

Three-Player Break with Two Defenders

Two defenders can be introduced and given practice in using the tandem defence. The two players going down the outside take the place of the two players who defended their attack, as shown in diagram 65.

Three versus Two and Two versus One

Three players break down the court, against two defenders, and aim to score. When the ball has been obtained by these two defenders, they break fast down to the other basket against one defender. The player who went down the middle on the three-versus-two phase becomes the defender in the two-versus-one situation. The other two attacking players become the next two defenders. In the two-versus-one phase, the man with the ball dribbles down the court to commit the one defender, only passing off when he has committed the defender (diagram 66).

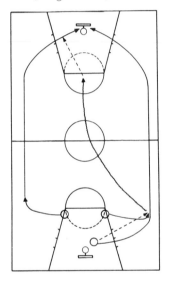 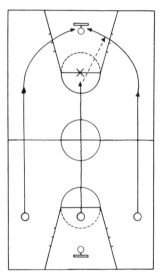

DIAGRAM 63   DIAGRAM 64

Continuous Fast Break —Three versus Two

This is a practice in which three players break fast down the court, and attack and score against two defenders. Once this attack has been completed, the two defenders are joined by one other player and they then break fast down to the other end, where two defenders are stationed. There is a waiting file of players at each end of the court at one side. After an attack, the attacking players join the end of a waiting file. As a new

fast break develops from one end, the next two players in the
file step out as the next defenders at the end (diagram 67).

Three-versus-Three Fast Break

Another fast break practice involving the need for an early
shot is the three-versus-three practice. In this practice three
players start the attack from one end, against two defenders at
the other end. The waiting players in this practice are
stationed at the half-way line. As the three offensive players
pass this' group, the first man in the group comes in behind
them as a third defender. Thus the three on attack have only

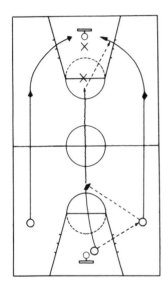

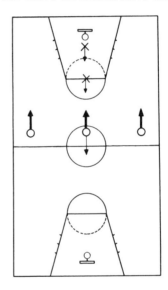

DIAGRAM 65   DIAGRAM 66

limited time with an overload situation. When the attack ends
with a score or loss of possession, the three defenders break
fast down to the other end. The next two waiting players come
out as defenders, to be joined, as in the previous attack, by the
next man in line, who moves in only after the attacking players
have moved past. This routine continues. In this fast break
practice the attacking players are looking for an early shot.

In all these fast break practices the coach must work for

controlled speed and the early shot, checking that the three lanes are filled on the break and on safe passing and dribbling. When players move to the final phase of the fast break, the ball should be in the middle lane and, unless he can go all the way, the middle player should stop at the D.

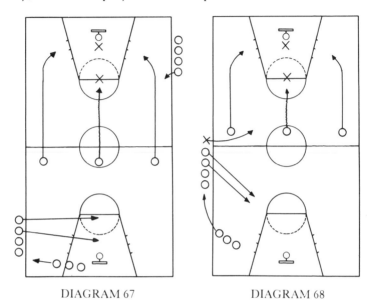

DIAGRAM 67   DIAGRAM 68

Glossary and Selective Index

Basketball, like other sports, has its own 'jargon' used to describe certain aspects of playing the game. Often a number of different names are given to the same action and, of course, many terms have their origin in the rules of the game. Most of the terms originating from the rules have been omitted and, where they are given, the fact that the term comes from the rules has been noted. Where more than one term is used, the most popular one has been defined. It is hoped that, through the use of a standard terminology, communication and understanding will be improved between coaches, players and officials.

Alive Offensive player who has the ball, but has not dribbled.

Assist A pass to an open team-mate that results in an immediate score.

Back court That half of the court which contains a team's defensive basket; vi.

Backdoor A term used to describe a cut by an offensive player towards the basket, to the side of the defensive player away from the ball. It is mainly used when the offensive player is being overplayed or when the defence turns to look at the ball or in another direction; 129.

Ball control game A type of offensive play that emphasises maintaining possession of the ball until a good shot is possible.

Ball hawk A player who is adept in recovering the ball either by intercepting a pass or by snapping up a loose ball.

Baseline drive A drive (q.v.) made close to the offensive end line of the court.

Blocking 'Is personal contact which impedes the progress of an opponent who is not in possession of the ball', (Rules article 77).

Blocking out (blocking off) (box out) (cut out) The positioning of the defensive player in such a manner as to prevent an offensive player from moving to the basket to gain a rebound; 105.

Box and one A term used to describe a combination defence (q.v.) with four men playing a zone defence (q.v.) in a square formation, (i.e. 2:2) with one man out chasing or marking a particular opponent.

Break The rapid movement of a player to a space where he hopes to receive a pass.

Brush-off (brush-off screen) To cause one's opponent to run into a third player thus 'losing' him momentarily; 86.

Buttonhook To move in one direction, turn sharply and double back.

Centre The name of one of the positions on the team, usually the tallest player in the team. The post player (q.v.).

Charging A personal foul caused by a player making bodily contact by running into an opponent. Usually committed by an offensive player.

Chaser A defender whose duty is to harass the offensive players, usually the front man or men in a zone defence (q.v.).

Circulation A player's movements about the court on offence.

Clear out An offensive manoeuvre in which players vacate an area of court, so as to isolate one offensive player and one defensive player. The offensive player may then attempt to score against his opponent, who has no defensive team-mates close enough to help him.

Combination defence A team defence in which some of the team play zone defence (q.v.) and others man-to-man defence (q.v.).

Continuity play A team offensive system in which men move to one position and then another in a regular order, executing pre-planned play options in an endeavour to create a scoring opportunity. The offensive players' movements on court are so planned that it is not necessary to set-up (q.v.) the offensive pattern after each play option has been attempted. The positioning of players after one play option has been attempted is used as the starting position for the next option.

Control basketball (possession basketball) A style of play in which a team deliberately makes sure of every pass and only shoots when there is a very high percentage chance of scoring.

Controlling the boards Gaining the majority of the rebounds.

Cut A quick movement by an offensive player without the ball to gain an advantage over the defence, usually directed towards the basket; 82.

Cutaway A player's move in cutting for basket after setting up a screen (q.v.) situation.

Cutter A player who cuts (q.v.) or breaks (q.v.); 101.

Dead An offensive player who has used his dribble.

Diamond and one A term used to describe a combination defence (q.v.), with four men playing a zone defence (q.v.) in a diamond formation (i.e. 1:2:1) with one man out chasing the ball or marking a particular opponent.

Drill A repetitive practice designed to improve one or more particular fundamental skills or team combinations.

Drive The movement of an offensive player while aggressively dribbling towards the basket in an attempt to score; 69.

Double team When two defensive players mark one opponent with the ball, usually a temporary measure (see Trap); 149.

Dunk A shot in which a jumping player puts the ball down into the opponent's basket from above.

Fake (feint) A movement made with the aim of deceiving an opponent; 75.

Fall-away A method of performing certain shots and passes in which the player with the ball moves in one direction as the ball moves in another.

Fast break (quick break) A fast offence that attempts to advance the ball to the front court before the defence is organised, with the object of achieving numerical superiority to give a good shot; 172

Feed To pass the ball to a team-mate who is in a scoring position.

Feint See Fake.

Floating A manoeuvre in man-to-man defence in which a defender marking an opponent on the weak side (q.v.) stays between his opponent and the basket, but, because the ball is on the opposite side of the court, moves laterally towards it; 102, 113.

Floor play Used to describe the movements on the court of players of either team.

Fouled out Being required to leave the game after committing five fouls.

Foul line Free throw line.

Forward The name of one of the positions in the team. The forwards play on offence in the area of court, either on the right- or left-hand side, between the restricted area (q.v.) and the side lines; vi, 159.

Free ball (loose ball) A ball which, although in play, is not in the possession of either team.

Freelance An unstructured type of offence in which players take advantage of whatever offensive opportunities arise.

Freezing the ball (stall) The action of a team in possession of the ball who attempt to retain possession of the ball without an attempt to score. Limited to 30 seconds and often used late in the game in an effort to protect a slight lead.

Front court That half of the court which contains the basket which a team is attacking; vi.

Fronting the post Guarding the post player (q.v.) in front, rather than between him and the basket. A defensive tactic aiming to prevent a good post player from receiving the ball close to the basket; 103.

Front screen A screen set up by an offensive player between a team-mate and his team-mate's opponent; 168.

Full-court press A pressing defence which operates throughout the whole court and not merely in the defender's back court (q.v.). See Press; 155_

Fundamentals The basic skills of the game, necessary as a background for all team play.

Give and go An offensive manoeuvre in which a player passes the ball to a team-mate and cuts (q.v.) towards basket for a return pass; 82, 128.

Guard (playmaker) (quarter-back) The name of one of the positions on the team, usually played by a shorter player, who on offence will play in the area of court between the centre line and the free throw line extended to the side lines; vi, 159.

Half-court press A pressing defence which operates in a team's back court.

Held ball '. . . is declared when two players of opposing teams have one or both hands firmly on the ball, or held ball may be called when one closely guarded player does not pass, shoot, bat, roll or dribble the ball within 5 seconds' (Rules, article 55).

High A position played by an offensive player who plays in the area of court away from the end line near to the free-throw line; 141.

In line The basic man-to-man defensive position 'in line' between the opponent and the basket being defended; 94.

Inside (1) In the area under the basket.
(2) Between the perimeter of the defence and the basket it is defending.
(3) 'inside' the key (q.v.).

Jump ball 'A jump ball takes place when the official tosses the ball between two opposing players' (Rules, article 26).

Key (keyhole) The restricted area (q.v.) including the circle, derived from the original keyhole shape.

Lane See Restricted area.

Lead pass A pass thrown ahead of the intended receiver, so that he can catch the ball on the move and maintain his speed.

Low A position held by an offensive player operating in the area of court near to the end line or basket.

Man-to-man defence A style of defence in which each player is assigned to guard a specific opponent regardless of where he goes in his offensive manoeuvres; 148.

Out-of-bounds The area outside the legal playing court, i.e. outside the inside edge of the lines marking the side lines and the end lines.

Off line A variation of 'in-line' defence (q.v.), in which the defender takes up a position slightly to one side of his opponent, but still between the opponent and the basket. The aim is to reduce the opponent's offensive options; 112.

One on one (1 v. 1) The situation where one offensive player attacks one defensive player; Chapter 3.

Options Alternative offensive manoeuvres that can occur in a game situation; 124.

Outlet pass The first pass made after a defensive rebound (q.v.), usually made to a player stationed near to the closest side line of the court and used to initiate a fast break (q.v.); 172.

Outside (1) Nearer the side line of the court.

(2) Between the side line and the perimeter of the defence.

(3) 'Outside' the key (q.v.)

Overload Outnumber; 171.

Overtime The extra period(s) played after the expiration of the second half of a game in which the score has been tied. Play is continued for an extra period of 5 minutes or as many such periods of 5 minutes as may be necessary to break the tie.

Pass and cut See Give and go.

Pattern The predetermined formation adopted by an offensive team prior to their initiating offensive manoeuvres. Common patterns are 1:3:1 and 2:3.

Pattern play Offensive plays initiated from fixed and predetermined court positions.

Pick (side-screen) A screen (q.v.) set at the side of a team-mate's opponent; 133.

Pick and roll A side screen followed by a pivot towards the basket by the player who has set the screen, useful against a switching man-to-man defence; 137.

Pivot (1) 'A pivot takes place when a player who is holding the ball steps once or more than once in any direction with the same foot, the other foot, called the pivot foot, being kept at its point of contact with the floor' (Rules, article 52); 61.

(2) Another name for a post player (q.v.).

Playmaker A player who is adept at setting up situations·that will enable team-mates to have a scoring opportunity. See also Guard.

Play A term used to describe a series of movements of players and/or the ball on court, mainly used for offensive manoeuvres.

Post (1) See post player; vi.

(2) An offensive manoeuvre in which a player takes up a position, usually with his back to the basket he is attacking, thus providing a target to receive a pass and/or act as a rear screen (q.v.) to enable team-mates to run their opponents into the post; 84, 139.

Post player Usually the tallest player in the team, who operates on offence in an area near the sides of, and occasionally in, the free throw lane and close to the basket. He is stationed there for scoring purposes and to feed cutters (q.v.), and is a player around whom the offensive team pivots. He is, therefore, sometimes called a pivot player; vi, 159.

Press A defensive attempt to force the opposing team into making some kind of error and thus lose possession of the ball. It is accomplished usually by aggressive defence, double teaming (q.v.) or harrassing the ball-handler with attempts to tie-up (q.v.) the ball. The press can be applied full court, half court or any other fractional part of the playing area and can be based on either man-to-man or zone (q.v.) principles; 148, 154.

Quarterback See Playmaker or Guard. A term derived from American football.

Quick break See Fast break.

Rebound A term used to describe the actual retrieving of the ball as it rebounds from the backboard or the ring after an unsuccessful shot. Offensive rebound therefore means gaining the rebound from the team's offensive basket (i.e. the one it is attacking). Defensive rebound is retrieving the ball from the team's defensive basket (i.e. the basket it is defending); 106.

Rebound triangle A term used to describe the positioning of a group of three defenders, who form a triangle around the basket, after a shot has been attempted. This is to cover the probable positions of the ball should a rebound occur and prevent an opponent from gaining a good position from which to collect the rebound.

Restraining circles The circles with 3.60 metres (12 feet) diameter located in the centre of the court and at the free throw lines.

Restricted areas 'The restricted areas shall be spaces marked in the court which are limited by the end lines, the free throw lines and by lines which originate at the end lines, their outer edges being 3 metres from the midpoints of the end lines, and terminate at the end of the free throw lines' (Rules, article 7).

Reverse (roll) A change of direction in which the offensive player endeavours to free himself from a close-marking defender. The change of direction is executed after a move towards the defender and a pivot, so that the offensive player turns his back on his opponent and then moves off in the new direction; 72, 83.

Safety man An offensive player who plays in the guard position, with the aim of defending against possible fast breaks on loss of possession and of receiving a pass when an offensive play breaks down; 121, 159.

Sag When a defender moves away from his opponent towards the basket he is defending; 102.

Sagging defence A team defensive tactic in which the defenders furthest from the ball sag away from their opponents, towards the basket, to help their team-mates and cover the high percentage scoring area; 113, 148.

Screen A screen occurs when an offensive player attempts to prevent a defender from reaching a desired position or maintain his defensive position. The screen is intended to impede the progress of the defender, so that the offensive player he is marking has an unimpeded shot or a clear path to basket; 84, 123, 133, 143.

Scrimmage A practice game.

Set play (1) A repetitive, pre-arranged form of offence.
(2) A play (q.v.) executed to predetermined and rehearsed moves, which, when applied at certain set situations in the game, is intended to result in a favourable scoring chance. The set situations are usually out-of-bounds, jump-ball or the free-throw situation.

Set-up The action of establishing an offensive pattern (q.v.) or the defensive organisation.

Series A name given to a number of plays used by an offensive team in particular situations, e.g. high post plays.

Slow break A deliberate attack against a defence that is set-up (q.v.).

Slide When a defensive player, in order to prevent himself being screened, moves, as he follows his own opponent, between a team-mate and that team-mate's opponent; 133.

Stall See Freezing the ball.

Steal To take the ball away from an opponent.

Strong side Refers to the side of the court on which the offensive team has the ball (at any one time).

Switch A defensive manoeuvre in which two defenders exchange defensive responsibilities by changing the men they are guarding. It occurs usually during a screen situation in which one of the defenders can no longer guard his man because of the screen; 136.

System A team's basic offensive and defensive plays.

Tie-Up A defensive situation in which the defenders, through their defensive tactics, gain a held ball (q.v.) situation.

Tip The momentary catching and pushing of the ball towards the basket, executed by an offensive rebounder in an attempt to score from an offensive rebound (q.v.) while he is still in the air; 46.

Tip-off The centre jump-ball at the start of play.

Trailer An offensive player who follows behind the ball-handler.

Trap A 'double team' (q.v.) in which two defenders attempt to stop a dribbler and prevent him from making a successful pass.

Transposition Occurs after the change of possession, as a team moves from offence to defence and vice versa; 125.

Turnover The loss of ball possession without there having been an attempt by the offensive team to shoot at basket.

Weak side The opposite side of the court to the strong side (q.v.), i.e. away from the ball; 102.

Zone defence A team's defensive tactic in which the five defensive players react to the ball and, in so doing, are each responsible for an area of the court in which they move in relation to the movements of the ball; 149.

GV
885
C593   Coleman, Brian E.
1975   Basketball